THE PRISONER AT LAEKEN

King Leopold with his three children.

Photograph taken by Queen Elisabeth and given to Admiral Sir Roger Keyes.

THE PRISONER
AT LAEKEN

KING LEOPOLD
Legend and Fact

BY

EMILE CAMMAERTS

With a Preface by

ADMIRAL OF THE FLEET
SIR ROGER KEYES, BT.,
G.C.B., K.C.V.O., C.M.G., D.S.O.

THE CRESSET PRESS

LONDON 1941

First published June, 1941
Second Impression June, 1941
Third Impression July, 1941
Fourth Impression July, 1941

Printed in Great Britain
by the SHENVAL PRESS

CONTENTS

PREFACE

THE FLOOD of poisonous abuse which was directed at King Leopold after the capitulation of the Belgian Army last May was, of course, inspired by certain Frenchmen seeking a scapegoat to cover their own failures and shortcomings.

It is difficult to overtake a lie and, although this calumny, which was widely believed at the time, has to a great extent died down in the light of the truth, unfair and ungenerous statements reappear from time to time. Monsieur Cammaerts is to be congratulated on having produced, in these pages, a wealth of evidence which should establish the truth and vindicate the honour of his King beyond all doubt.

As I was with King Leopold at the Headquarters of his Army throughout the brief campaign in Belgium, and at the same time in close touch with the Headquarters of the British Army and Government, I had unrivalled opportunities of observing the course of events. I am glad to have this opportunity of declaring that King Leopold was steadfast in his loyalty to the Allies and did everything in his power to help their Armies.

I first met King Leopold in 1918 when his parents, King Albert and Queen Elisabeth, lived at La Panne, within range of the enemy, under cover of the guns of the Dover Patrol, which I commanded. King Leopold was then a schoolboy, and he spent his holidays as a private in the 9th Infantry, which was often in action in the Belgian front-line trenches.

A few hours after the Germans invaded Belgium on the 10th May 1940, at the request of the Government, I left by aeroplane to join King Leopold as special liaison officer.

I remained with him until 10 p.m. on the night of the 27th May.

The King's bearing was always calm and courageous under the heavy blows he and his people suffered through the treachery of Germany and the failure of the French to prevent the German armoured columns from forcing the Meuse at Sedan, and threatening the right flank of the allied French-British-Belgian Army in the northward.

King Leopold had placed himself and his Army under the French High Command. In accordance with the orders he received, and conforming to the movements of the French Northern Army and the British Army, the Belgian Army had to retire day after day until it reached the Scheldt, where it was hoped that a final stand would be made. The Belgian G.H.Q. was established at St. André outside Bruges and I stayed with King Leopold at Lophem nearby, later at Wynendael.

On the 20th May, the French High Command ordered the British and French Armies to prepare to fight to the south-westward, to regain contact with the main French Army to the southward. I was at the British G.H.Q. at Wahagnies when these orders were received and it was generally recognised that the abandonment of the Belgian Army was inevitable, unless it could conform to this movement.

On my return to the Belgian G.H.Q. I told King Leopold of the instructions Lord Gort had received, and said that it was hoped by my Government that the Belgian Army would conform and keep contact with the left flank of the British Army.

The King of the Belgians asked me to inform the British Government and Lord Gort, that the Belgian Army existed solely for defence and possessed neither tanks nor aircraft, nor the equipment for offensive warfare. Owing to the influx of refugees, not more than fourteen days' food remained in the small part of Belgium left to him. He did not feel that he had any right to expect the British Government to consider jeopardising, perhaps, the very existence of the British Army in order to keep contact with the Belgian Army. He asked me to make it clear that he did not wish to do anything to interfere with any action which the British Government might consider it desirable for the British Army to undertake towards the southward. He asked me to say, however, that he fully realised that such action would finally lead to the separation of the two Armies and, in this event, the capitulation of the Belgian Army would be inevitable.

I sent a telegram to this effect to the Prime Minister and Lord Gort, and I gave a copy to Lord Gort, personally, the next day.

On the 21st May, I was with King Leopold at Ypres when he met General Weygand, the new General-issimo of the Allied Armies. General Weygand confirmed the orders which had been given to the French and British Armies on 20th May, and requested King Leopold to withdraw from the Scheldt to the Lys, in one behind the Lys. At the same time he sent the 68th French Division—one of the two French divisions which were in reserve on the Belgian left flank and under his orders—across the Yser in Belgian buses and lorries to Gravelines. The only Allied troops left in Belgium were the 60th French Division.

On 24th May General Weygand told the Commanders of the British Army and French Northern Army that the advance of the French Army from the southwards was going well, and he ordered them to attack vigorously to the southwards in order to close the gap behind the German Panzer divisions which had broken through to the coast.

By this time the Belgian Army was heavily engaged and it was evident to the Belgian G.H.Q. that they were faced with an attack by eight or nine German divisions with the object of driving the Belgian Army to the northward and severing its contact with the British Army, which was now lying behind its winter line on the frontier.

It was clear to us on the spot that the dangers and difficulties of the situation were not realized by the French High Command and, in response to an urgent request, General Dill, British C.I.G.S., came over on the evening of the 24th. After staying the night with the British Mission he visited Lord Gort's Headquarters at Premesque on the following morning.

On his return to Bruges he told King Leopold that the attack to the southward by the French and British Armies, as ordered by General Weygand, would be carried out.

King Leopold showed General Dill on the map the

weak spot on the Belgian right flank, the weakness of their defence line generally,[1] and the impossibility of holding it and also keeping contact, unless strong help could be provided by the British Army. General Dill promised to ask Lord Gort to do what he could to help contact being maintained.

As the British Army was about to attack to the southward, the King felt that he could best help by keeping touch as long as possible with its left flank. He had already withdrawn his mechanized cavalry division from the left flank on the coast to reinforce the right flank, and he now gave orders for the 15th Division (infantry with no artillery nor machine guns) from the Yser further to reinforce that flank. This exhausted all his reserves.

I learned later that the British 5th Division was then ordered to move to the northward to occupy the line from Halluin to Zillebeke and the 12th Lancers to support the Allied flanks. This helped to cover the British left flank, but did not effectively ease the situation for the Belgian Army, which, in the King's great effort to help the B.E.F., was strung out from Halluin to the sea on a front of 90 kilometres, and was threatened by German attacks at several points.

Fearing a break-through by the Germans to be inevitable, the Belgians had been collecting rolling stock and massing it along the railways between Roulers and Ypres, and to the southward, to form a barrier to delay the advance of enemy armoured troops to the northward.

On the morning of the 26th, on learning of the heavy attacks towards Ypres, and the imminence of a break in the Belgian line, I went to our G.H.Q. at Premesque to ask Lord Gort if there was anything I could do to help. He asked me to urge King Leopold to withdraw the Belgian Army towards the Yser.

I gave this message to the King, who said they would do their best, but the only way of averting an imminent and complete disaster was for an immediate British counter-attack between the Lys and the Scheldt. I telegraphed this to Lord Gort and found that similar appeals had been conveyed by the British Mission from the Belgian G.H.Q. by telegram and despatch rider since an early hour that morning.

The question of the Belgian Army retiring to the Yser, if it was forced to fall back from the Lys, had been considered at the Conference at Ypres on 21st May. At that time King Leopold thought this might be the only alternative line, but the recent German thrust, the whole brunt of which had fallen on the Belgians, had, he feared, made a withdrawal to the Yser impracticable.

The King told me later in the day, 26th May, that he had discussed the matter with his General Staff, who considered that a withdrawal to the Yser was a physical impossibility under the pressure the enemy were exerting. A withdrawal over roads thronged with refugees, without adequate fighter cover, would be costly and would only end in disaster; moreover, it would mean the abandonment of all their ammunition, stores and food.

On the other hand, his G.H.Q. declared that a British counter-attack on the vulnerable flank of the enemy must be undertaken if a disaster was to be averted, and that the opportunity might only last a few more hours.

They were insistent that the British Army, on its well-prepared defence line between Halluin and Bourghelles, was well placed, on the flank of the enemy, to strike at his communications and bridge-heads on the Scheldt and the Lys, with every prospect of inflicting a considerable defeat on him, and relieving the pressure on the Belgian Army.

An officer from the British Mission was sent to G.H.Q. that evening to explain the Belgian views.

Having no reserves of his own, King Leopold gave orders for the remaining French 60th Division to be taken in Belgian vehicles to a prepared position across the Yser, which had by now been flooded over a wide area, and its bridges mined.[1]

The King remarked to me that if the British Army had been preparing to attack to the south-westward, as he had been informed, it would be difficult for it to mount an attack towards the eastward, in time to prevent the Belgian right flank being crushed and its line overwhelmed.

But the British Army was in no better condition to deliver the counter-attack for which the G.H.Q. pleaded, than the Belgian Army was to disengage and withdraw to the Yser as demanded by Lord Gort.

[1] This order was carried out the next morning, according to arrangements made with General Champon, Head of the French Mission. If this division was moved from this position, the Belgians cannot be rendered responsible for the change. General Champon had established his Headquarters at La Panne and was in sole Command of the French troops remaining in Belgium.—A.

Although King Leopold did not know at that time, and no message to this effect ever reached him, Lord Gort had already received orders to withdraw to the coast and was preparing to do so.

Meanwhile the fighting on the Belgian front had been continuous for four days and the Belgian Army, short of food and ammunition, had withstood a tremendous onslaught from eight German divisions, including several armoured units supported by wave after wave of dive bombers. Fighting with great gallantry, the Belgians had delivered several counter-attacks, slain some thousands of Germans and taken several hundred prisoners, but they were nearing the end of their resistance.

On the morning of the 27th May, King Leopold asked me to tell Lord Gort that he feared a moment was rapidly approaching when he could no longer rely on his troops to fight or be of further use to the British Army. He would be obliged to surrender before a débâcle. He fully appreciated that the British Army had done everything in its power to help Belgium, and he asked Lord Gort to believe that he had done everything in his power to avert this catastrophe.

I sent this message by wireless to Lord Gort, as all telephone communications had been cut, but I understand he did not receive it.

At that time King Leopold hoped to be able to hold out for another day, but by the afternoon the German Army had driven a wedge between the Belgian and British Armies and pierced the line in two or three places. Every road, village and town in the small part of Belgium left in Belgian hands was thronged with hundreds of thousands of refugees, and they and the troops were being mercilessly bombed by low-flying aircraft.

Knowing that he could do nothing further to help his Allies, King Leopold told me and the British and French Missions at his G.H.Q. that he intended to ask for an armistice at midnight in order to avoid further slaughter of his sorely-tried people.

The British Mission informed the War Office by wireless, and the message was received in London at 5.54 p.m., but all efforts to get in touch with our G.H.Q. failed.[1]

King Leopold had been asked by his Government. and ours, to leave his country and to carry on the war from without, but he told me that, as Commander-in-Chief of his Army, which was fighting a desperate battle, he must share the fate of his troops. His mother, Queen Elisabeth, was with him throughout these last days and elected to share his captivity.

The King told me that he realized his position would be very difficult, but he would use every endeavour to prevent his countrymen from being compelled to associate themselves with any action against the countries which had attempted to help Belgium in her plight.

As the King and the Queen refused to accompany me

---

[1] General Champon stated that he had been unable to communicate with General Blanchard, whose Headquarters had been moved, but that he had succeeded in making contact with General Weygand by radio. See p. 19.—A.

to England, and the enemy were close to Bruges, I took my leave of Their Majesties at 10 p.m. on the 27th, and made my way to Nieuport, where I was picked up by a motor torpedo boat just before dawn on the 28th May.

As is now well known, King Leopold made no separate peace, and is a prisoner of war.

Misfortune has thus overwhelmed his country for a second time in his life, but the Belgians may well be proud of their King, for he has proved himself to be a gallant soldier, a loyal ally and a true son of his splendid parents.

ROGER KEYES

TINGEWICK HOUSE,
  BUCKINGHAM,
    May, 1941.

INTRODUCTION

ALMOST EVERY human conception is the result of a combination of observation and imagination. In studying nature, the scientist has to guard himself against errors because his mind may easily be waylaid by preconceptions or hasty conclusions. In historical or social studies, the chances of such errors are considerably increased by the fact that both the student and the object of his studies are a compound of accurate and inaccurate factors. Illusion spreads from the observer to the observed or vice versa, and distorts the outline or the proportions of the picture. History, as the strictly faithful record of actual facts, and legend, as the embellishment or vilification of these facts, stand at opposite poles of the human mind. Nothing happens, however, in the life of the individual or of the community in which these two aspects of knowledge are not to a certain extent reflected. Some trifling incident may be the origin of the most poetical or dramatic legend and, on the other hand, there are few pages of history, even of modern history, from which legend may be said to be completely excluded.

In this book I have tried to record most of the material which will provide either the legend or the "history" of King Leopold. This record is a first attempt to sift the evidence at present available in order to separate the legendary from the historical elements of the story, and to prepare the ground for a just appreciation of its central figure.

It is a common belief that legends could only grow

in ancient days when the mind of man was like that of a child, prone to wander from the path of truth. Thinking of Greek or German mythologies or of mediæval lore, we are inclined to eliminate legends from modern times. We point out that contemporary records should be more reliable than old poems or chronicles based on oral tradition, handed down from one generation to another and which must necessarily alter in the process. We overlook the fact that these records, just because they deal with topical events, may give a distorted picture of them and that, in times of crisis, even the most educated people are apt to spread the wildest rumours. Neither can we respect the printed word as such, in the light of some of the information published in the Press. Instead of controlling the human tendency towards blind confidence or blinder suspicion, some papers often stimulate them by sensational comments or baseless exaggerations. Sound news does not always make "good copy".

Legends have always flourished in wartime because fear and its reaction, courage, stimulate the imagination. King Arthur, King Alfred, Charlemagne, Napoleon have all been the central figures of cycles of legendary traditions. The "Napoleonic legend" which has been studied with so much care during the last fifty years, may not be as valuable, from the literary point of view, as the *Iliad*, the *Chanson de Roland*, or the *Morte d'Arthur*, but it contains all the elements which characterize these epics. In most of them the figure of the hero is strongly opposed to the figure of the traitor who brings about his downfall. Roland would not be complete without Ganelon, Siegfried without Hagen,

Arthur without Mordred. Belief in invincibility implies belief in treachery, for only through treason can the true hero's virtue be surprised.

The last war also had its traitor—the Kaiser—and, for a short time, its hero—King Albert. Soon, however, the stage became too crowded to allow the development of a simple story. Interest spread to many lands and leaders and the issue was confused. But popular imagination exerted itself nevertheless. We had Russian contingents landing in Scotland on their way to France, the Angels of Mons, and, last but not least, the German "corpse factory" on the Western front. The latter discovery, which exposed the callous brutality of the enemy, was duly reported in Lord Northcliffe's *The Times*, with appropriate comments, and it was only a few weeks later that someone pointed out that the word used for these gruesome works was *Kadaver* (carcass) and not *Leichnam* (corpse).

This shows, however, that, if legends are apt to grow as quickly and profusedly in modern days as they did in the past, they are more likely to be exposed. Illusions are still with us, but beside the power of creating them, we possess to a higher degree than our forefathers the power of destroying them. Legends which were allowed to thrive unhindered are soon opposed nowadays either by a disinterested love of truth or by the spirit of criticism prevalent in intellectual circles. "Debunking" has recently done a certain amount of harm by vainly trying to lower the stature of men of genius who deserve the admiration they receive, but it has also done a certain amount of good by removing undeserved blemishes which soiled the reputation of other public men. The horse of fantasy is no longer allowed to run wild through the fields of Time. There are too many trainers about, eager to capture it and to test its strength. Art may lose through their ceaseless activity, but history will undoubtedly benefit from it.

It is noticeable that practically every war-legend rests on some slender foundation. The arrival of the "Russians", in the winter of 1914, coincided with the use of sheepskins which, for the first time, were added to the soldiers' equipment. It has been suggested that some of the newly formed Scottish regiments travelled, no doubt, from Ross-shire to London on their way to France. This would give us all the conditions required for the successful development of the story: during a tense crisis, an element of truth distorted by some misconception and encouraged by wishful thinking. The same wishful thinking which creates imaginary reinforcements transforms a local success into a victory or a serious defeat into a strategic retreat. Imagination heightens the virtue of friends and deepens the wickedness of foes. Sacrifice becomes martyrdom and simple courage, unique heroism. The trustworthy record of arson and massacres has to be made still more horrible by fantastic tales of torture and mutilation. Every carcass becomes a corpse.

If mention has been made of the angels who were supposed to have saved a British regiment during the retreat from Mons, it is not on account of the supernatural, but of the natural character of the story. There are, no doubt, many supernatural events which are historically trustworthy. All Christians should recognize this fact. But when they arise in the midst of a battle and more particularly when they are the outward sign of an alliance between God and one of the belligerents against the other, they should be received with the greatest caution. It is almost too easy and somewhat blasphemous to enlist the Divinity among one's allies. Constantine is supposed to have done it and Clovis, the King of the Franks: *In hoc signo vinces*. Conversion became the price of victory in Christian times, as sacrifice had been the price of victory in pagan times. There is no appreciable difference between Agamemnon's action in sacrificing Iphigenia and some barbarian chief's resolution to burn his old idols and worship the true God. Angels are not used to fight men, they are used to fight demons, as in the Revelation, or to gather men's souls as in the *Chanson de Roland*. Such angels will always be remembered, the others are passing visions which disappear as soon as the danger is over—like the angels of Mons.

*   *   *   *

If the legend-creating power was particularly active during the last War, it should have been still more active in the present one. The nervous tension was if anything greater, and had been preceded by a long period of doubt and anxiety—including the crisis of September 1938—beside which the period of 1904–1914 appears like a time of calm confidence. The clash between totalitarianism and democracy is still more uncompromising than the conflict between national interests. The last war was waged for or against the conquest of the hegemony in Europe. The present war is waged for or against the conquest of hegemony in the world. In 1914, the Reich violated international law and proclaimed the supremacy of Might over Right as a means to achieve its end. In 1939, the Reich adopted the violation of international order as a regular policy. It became an end in itself, the rule of one man, of one system, being violently and blatantly opposed to the rule of law. In 1914, the issue was mainly political; in 1939, it was mainly ideological. In this country at least, the last struggle did not rally at first the unanimous support of the people. There remained to the end an influential minority who opposed it. The same could not be said to-day. All through the anxious years which preceded the conflict, public opinion, instead of lagging behind the Government, was inclined to force the pace. It took all the prestige enjoyed by Mr. Chamberlain and the discipline of his large majority to allow him to pursue to the bitter end his policy of appeasement.

For all these reasons, we should have expected, from the beginning of hostilities, an imaginative outburst productive of a large number of picturesque if doubtful stories. Legends, however, were few and far between during the first eight months. Wishful thinking manifested itself, no doubt. People sought comfort in inspecting the formidable defences of the Maginot Line in picture theatres, and in the fond belief that these defences had been prolonged as far as the sea. Others spoke of some mysterious weapon which would prevent any enemy raider from crossing the coast and of the strange contrivances installed to that effect which they had, of course, seen with their own eyes. Others again enlarged on the efficiency of the blockade and fixed the date when Germany, deprived of some essential material, would be compelled to sue for peace. But somehow popular imagination was not stirred to its depth. This war had not come as had the last, like a bolt from the blue. It had been expected for so long that its outbreak relieved rather than exasperated the nervous tension. Besides, it had begun in Poland, far away from these shores, and the long period of relative calm which followed the short Polish campaign had only been interrupted by submarine and anti-submarine warfare, and by the monotonous patrolling activity on the French frontier. All remained quiet on the Western front. Nothing happened in the "phoney war". Some people even began to believe that nothing would happen and that it would be enough for the Allies to sit tight and to pursue their economic warfare, while Soviet Russia watched complacently the downfall of Nazism and reaped the benefit of the Russo-German pact. Italy, we were assured, would never come in and would continue to sit on the fence.

This was not a fertile soil for the growth of legends. Nothing can be made of nothing. The cynics declared themselves bored and the idealists prepared their plans and wove their Utopias. Federalism and other systems were discussed in their smallest details and the future of the world was settled in a series of ponderous volumes.

Then suddenly came the conquest of Norway, the flash at Narvik and, before people had time to grasp the significance of the Allied reverse in the North, the blow fell on Holland and Belgium, on the very gate of Britain and France.

Never was a military campaign fought in such an atmosphere of unreality. It was as if the pent-up imaginative energy of the eight previous months had been suddenly released. Innate British optimism combined with French pessimism to spread the wildest illusions. For French pessimism had to be checked by the censorship in order to prevent an already growing nervous depression from floundering into defeatism. This was the most crucial moment in the history of mankind, a direct challenge to Liberalism, Humanism, Christian values. All the work accomplished during the last centuries was threatened with annihilation. To the Christian, this threat was paganism, to the trade-unionist slavery, to the scholar deliberate obscurantism, to the lawyer lawlessness, to the free citizen herd instinct. Nothing comparable had happened since the days of Charles Martel and Attila.

Propaganda is a double-edged weapon, as Nazism may still have to learn to its cost. For eight months, a belief in Allied preparedness had been fostered in order to bring comfort at home and to prevent doubtful neutrals—more particularly Italy—from throwing in their lot with Hitler. We had been told again and again that every month gained hammered another nail in his coffin, that the Reich's war production having reached its peak in 1939, must necessarily decrease in the following year, while Allied war production, owing to superior resources, was gaining in relative strength from month to month. Under-estimation, on the one side, and over-estimation, on the other, had gradually transformed a defensive into an offensive attitude. Whatever political or military leaders might have thought at the time, the people thought that the hour had struck. Ever since the invasion of Norway, they had grown more and more impatient at the obstacle erected in the West by the neutral barrier of Holland and Belgium. They wished to forestall the expected assault and to seize the initiative. Thinking of numbers more than of equipment, unable to appreciate the power of the new mechanized and aerial warfare as compared with the land operations of the last war, they welcomed the outbreak of May 10th as the starting point of a crushing victory which would shorten the duration of the war and put an end to their doubts and anxieties.

This was more than wishful thinking, it was a legend which, when the blow was struck, became almost a creed. It could not be questioned without awaking suspicions as to the questioner's loyalty and patriotism. Its dramatic collapse was bound to provoke an equally dramatic reaction. The dogma of invincibility is not destroyed in a day. When confronted with brutal and cruel facts it demands and, if necessary, invents explanations. Popular indignation cannot be allayed with the dismissal of a few military leaders, scapegoats must be found which will bear the responsibility of past mistakes. Every alien becomes a spy, defeat is turned into treason. This is the natural recoil of the weapon of propaganda. Old legends, when exploded, must breed new ones. Confusion becomes worse confounded.

This crude analysis implies no criticism. One of the worst features of war is that it is waged not on a philosophy of intentions, but on a philosophy of results. Its sense of justice is blind to certain evidence and deaf to certain explanations. It ignores the element of chance. Success, whether deserved or not, is hailed as virtue, and failure as sin. When fighting for their lives people are in no mood to consider every facet of the problem submitted to them. They jump at conclusions and, when these conclusions satisfy their self-complacency, they are naturally reluctant to alter them. This state of mind has prevailed in all times and all countries. It was particularly marked during the French Revolution, and, more recently, during the Russian and German Revolutions. In the worst circumstances, it unloosens terrorism, in the best circumstances, it provokes calumny.

*   *   *   *

If the "war of nerves" had failed to shake Britain's confidence in herself, it had been more successful in France, where public opinion was divided and where a strong Communist opposition had to be suppressed. M. Daladier's power never rested on a genuinely united front, and the strategy of General Gamelin was the object of some criticism. The prestige of the Maginot Line, and especially of its "prolongation to the sea", grew with the distance which extended behind it and with the ignorance of the experts who extolled its impregnability. Even during the first months of static warfare, French politicians did not hesitate to exploit these doubts in order to further their own interests or those of their party, and the breach between Right and Left was only apparently mended. The position of M. Daladier had never been a strong one, that of M. Reynaud, who replaced him after the

Allied reverse in Norway, was still more precarious. Nervousness fostered division and division fostered nervousness. In spite of the effort of officially controlled information and of a particularly severe censorship—or perhaps on account of them—an atmosphere of suspicion prevailed in Paris. All kinds of rumours spread abroad, some of them incriminating the ability and even the loyalty of some members of the Government.

The history of these critical weeks cannot yet be written. We shall, no doubt, be able to understand one day why General Gamelin altered his plans from the defensive to the offensive. The riddle of the well-prepared offensive of May 10th, launched by the French and British army corps massed on the Belgian frontier will likewise receive a more adequate justification than the desire to help the Dutch or to answer the appeal made by Belgium to the guarantor Powers. It is difficult to explain on the information available how the Generalissimo's overcautious defensive strategy was suddenly transformed into a reckless offensive in which the obvious precaution of protecting the hinge around which the turning movement was executed, seems to have been ignored. Up to the present, General Gamelin's military policy remains a mystery. So does General Weygand's, whose plan to re-establish the Allies' common front by a powerful counter-offensive vanished in smoke as soon as it was formulated. It may not have been practicable, but, if so, why did the new Generalissimo take so much trouble to advertise it? M. Reynaud's position is less difficult to understand. He had come to power on the understanding that he would wage war with the utmost energy, and must have realized from the first the terrible risks involved, owing to the Allies' marked inferiority in mechanized units and to the enemy's superiority in the air. He could rely neither on the wisdom of his generals, nor on the loyalty of some of his colleagues. After narrowly escaping defeat in the Chamber, he was only able to retain power owing to the outbreak of the *Blitzkrieg*. His situation was tragic in the extreme. If he hid the terrible truth after the break-through at Sedan, endorsing the official communiqués, he made himself the accomplice of a deliberate delusion in the hour of his country's greatest need. Being a patriot and a courageous man, he decided to make a clean breast of it in his ominous speech to the Senate on May 22nd. He remembered, no doubt, the great days of the French Revolution: *La Patrie en danger*, and Danton's rallying cry: *De l'audace, de l'audace, encore de l'audace, et la France est sauvée*! He decided to use every means available in order to steel the resistance of the army and of the people. He boldly dismissed Gamelin and a score of generals and called in Pétain and Weygand, the great leaders of the last war, the heirs of Foch's glory. He tried to galvanize the energy of his Cabinet by denouncing incompetence and criminal negligence. He declared that he would fight to the last ditch, in the last corner of France, at a time when people were already saying openly that further resistance was useless. When things went from bad to worse, in Paris and at the front, he called for a miracle, for another Marne. He was faced instead, on the 27th, by the surrender of the Belgian Army.

Something happened during that fatal night, while

INTRODUCTION

the French Premier, now at the end of his physical
and moral endurance, was preparing the speech
which he broadcast early the next day. Some say that
he lost his head, which would account for the fact that
he spoke twice of Leopold II instead of Leopold III.
He certainly lost his sense of justice for he had been
informed of the terrible plight in which the Belgian
Army was placed, and knew that the King, as Commander-in-Chief, intended to remain with his men.
Was the evident suggestion of betrayal the result of
over-excitement or the cool calculation of a leader who,
seeing that all other means are failing him, seizes this
last chance in the hope that bitterness might prove a
stronger stimulant than devotion? What matter the
reputation of a single man if France be saved!

"King Leopold, without warning General Blanchard, without one thought, without one word for the
British and French soldiers who came to the help of his
country on his anguished appeal, King Leopold II (III)
of the Belgians laid down his arms. It is a fact without
precedence in history". Most Belgians who heard these
terrible words felt the lash striking across their
shoulders. They sensed either a deliberate slander or a
monstrous misunderstanding, but they were unable, at
the time, to expose the first or to dispel the second.
Like the French, like the British, they had been led to
believe that their army was still intact, that the position of the Allies in the North, although grave, was
"not desperate". Even if Weygand's famous counter-
offensive were to fail, and it seemed certainly unduly
delayed, the Germans who had penetrated the Allied
lines as far as the sea were surely not strong enough to

xxxi

prevent the forty divisions engaged in Flanders and Northern France from joining the bulk of the French Army on the Somme. No one had yet spoken of evacuation. We were faced with the evident risks, but also with the chances, of a "war of movement", its success in one sector and its reverse in another. Apart from a small circle of allied leaders, no one realized, on May 28th, that the enveloping movement was complete, that the "iron ring" mentioned in the German communiqués constituted an insuperable obstacle, that by far the largest number of French and Belgian divisions were so exhausted that they were no longer able to resist the enemy's attacks, and that even the British suffered from a severe shortage in food and munitions.

It is against that dark background of misinformation that the effect of M. Reynaud's lurid words must be gauged. One legend breeds another. If the Belgian Army which had assumed the mission of covering the movements of the British and French towards the South was still well equipped and full of fight, according to the reports published at the time, if the King's orders, instead of being greeted with relief, caused widespread protests and were even ignored by a large number of his soldiers who "insisted on pursuing the struggle", then his action had neither excuse nor justification. If, on the other hand, his troops had reached the very limit of endurance, if all available reserves had been used up, if the Belgians, separated from the British, with their backs to the sea and every line of retreat cut off, were on the very brink of collapse, then surrender was both inevitable and justifiable.

*   *   *   *

There were other considerations which confused the issue and strengthened public belief in the legend of the King's treason: his refusal to leave his army and to follow his Ministers to London, the fact that "General Blanchard" had not received due warning of his decisions. These questions will be fully examined in the following chapters. They should not take our attention from the crux of the problem, the main cause of the indignation which branded the King of the Belgians as a traitor: after calling the Allies to his help, he had deliberately chosen to desert their ranks at the very moment when his desertion would bring about their downfall. At a time when his troops were still able to render the greatest services and perhaps to retrieve the situation, he had ordered them to lay down their arms, and thus "exposed the flank" of the British Expeditionary Force to the enemy's attack.

The full implications of M. Reynaud's words were soon realized. The Allies had purposely been drawn into Belgium, their generous support had brought them into a well prepared trap. The Belgians might be innocent, but the culpability of their King was only too evident. Had he not urged his people, in October, 1936, to leave the side of the Allies and to resume a position of neutrality in order to pacify Hitler? Had he not, without consulting Parliament, assumed personal command of the Army, on May 10th, in order that no one else could interfere with his plan? Why did the Belgians neglect to blow up the bridges on the Albert Canal? Why did they retire from the strong positions they occupied on the line Antwerp-Namur? Why did so many refugees encumber the roads, impeding military movements? Why was France led to believe that Belgian preparations and fortified works rendered useless the prolongation of the Maginot Line on the Franco-Belgian frontier? Did not Leopold "prevent them" from completing this line and "interfere with their defences" before the War? Was he not at heart anti-democratic and was not his entourage permeated with anti-French, pro-German and pro-Italian influences? No wonder that he refused to leave Belgium to come over to England where he would have been called upon to render a strict account of his actions, and that he preferred to accept the castle placed at his disposal by the Führer who would no doubt reward him for his outstanding services. . .

Many more things were said and written at the time, but we are concerned here with the core, not with the trimmings, of the legend. The storm let loose by M. Reynaud's speech in France spread to Britain and to America. It raged during the retreat on Dunkirk and only abated somewhat after the evacuation had proved successful, and after those who had taken part in the fighting were able to give a more accurate account of the military operations. It calmed down when the French disasters dispelled once for all the illusions entertained on French preparedness. The arrival in London of the Belgian Government, in October 1940, and the news which reached this country from Belgium, showing that the great majority of the Belgians remained loyal to their Sovereign, have since done a great deal to put a stop to these attacks. But, in spite of the disclosures made by a number of British, American and Belgian trustworthy witnesses, in spite of the belated publication of conclusive evidence, the whole story still leaves, to use a familiar expression, a bad taste in the mouth.

It takes a short time to destroy a great historic building or a noble reputation. It takes a long time to restore them. *"Calomniez,"* says Basile, *"il en restera toujours quelque chose."* Although the legend of King Leopold's treason has been exploded, the habit of associating him with well-known fifth columnists remains with us. The picture of the King of the Belgians no longer appears between those of Laval, Degrelle and Quisling, but his name is still sometimes coupled with theirs. Many people are too busy, in wartime, to reexamine past events in the light of new evidence. Their mind is preoccupied with what they consider to be more important things.

Unless the principles of truth and justice for which we are fighting are losing their hold on our consciousness, there are few more important things than to repair an injustice and to expose an untruth which have brought with them suffering, not only to their victim, but to millions of others. Belgium is still a constitutional monarchy and the vast majority of the Belgian people are as loyal and devoted to their Sovereign as the British people are to theirs. They shared the glory enjoyed, twenty-five years ago, by King Albert, they shared also the humiliation inflicted, a year ago, upon his son, and they will only raise their heads again when the last shadow of this humiliation has been removed and when a true appreciation of the facts dispels the false legends which have distorted them.

Before closing this introduction, I wish to forestall two criticisms. The first will be made by those who think that this book is not wanted, because the campaign of slander directed against the King of the Belgians was shortlived, and because "all well-informed people" know very well by now that it was unfounded.

I answer that, although this may be the impression of some of my readers, a much larger number who heard the indictment are not yet fully informed of the facts which contradict it. While I am writing, articles still appear in certain papers, entitled "Leopold The Damned," and scurrilous books on the subject are still in circulation. I am not battering at an open door. The door is only half open, and I wish to open it wide and to keep it wide open.

The second criticism will be that it is better, in these busy days, to "leave well alone", to let the dead bury the dead, and to allow Time to do its work.

I do not share this optimism. Neither Belgium, nor her King, nor his enemies, are dead yet, and the legend of 1940, if not dispelled, may do a great deal of harm in the near future. A prudent silence would be interpreted as a confession of defeat. It may be wise to leave well alone, but it is most dangerous to leave ill alone. Time works upon human beliefs as it works upon seeds. If they are good, they grow and bring forth fruit; if they are bad, they rot and breed corruption. E. C.

RADLETT.
March 1941.

Chapter I

M. REYNAUD'S INDICTMENT

THE STARTING-POINT of the campaign launched against King Leopold, the origin of the legend which has coupled his name with that of the worst type of fifth columnist, is the speech delivered by M. Reynaud on May 28th, 1940. Had this speech been worded differently, had it been made by any one but the French Premier whose trustworthiness was above suspicion, it would never have produced the same effect. France denounced Belgium. Between a powerful ally whose economic and political system was already closely linked with that of this country in the great struggle they were waging together, and a small neutral state which had only joined the Allies under pressure of dire necessity, British public opinion did not hesitate for one moment. The same inevitable choice was made between the reputation of the brilliant and pugnacious leader of the French Republic and that of the young Sovereign who had recently been criticized for his "neutralism" and faint-heartedness. The one could make himself heard all over the world, the other was reduced to silence. Besides, the facts spoke for themselves. M. Reynaud was still at the head of a free France and proclaimed his resolution to fight to the end. King Leopold had laid down his arms and delivered himself into the hands of the enemy. In the light of what happened in Norway and in Holland, the explanation suggested by the French Premier was only too plausible. From the partisans of Quisling, to the influential Germans and pro-Germans in Rotterdam and to the Head of the Belgian nation, there was a gradual and dramatic progression which most people followed unquestioningly.

A number of interesting books have been written on the collapse of France, notably by Alexander Werth, André Maurois and Elie Bois. In the light of the information they provide, it would not be difficult to-day to turn the tables against M. Reynaud. We may wonder why he consented to retain in his Cabinet men who did not share his views on the defence of the country and on the best methods of achieving it. Was M. Reynaud driven into this false position by his own personal ambition or by the intrigues of his entourage? Was not his anger against King Leopold considerably increased by the fact that, as French Premier, he had pressed General Gamelin to launch the Allied offensive through Belgium and Holland on May 10th, and to depart from the defensive strategy pursued hitherto? And did he take this course, as M. Maurois suggests, because he knew that his political fate depended on a "bold and vigorous" prosecution of the war?

It would be only too easy to make capital out of the evidence produced against M. Reynaud during the last months, but since he has not yet been able to answer his critics, I shall only examine here one by one every item of his indictment against King Leopold on its own merits.

1. *"The Anguished Appeal"*

"Eighteen days ago," said M. Reynaud, "this same King addressed to us an appeal for help. To that appeal we responded, following a plan conceived by the Allied General Staffs last December." And further, "without one word, without one thought for the British and French soldiers who came to the help of his country on his *anguished appeal*, King Leopold III of the Belgians laid down his arms."

The appeal for help was particularly insisted upon because it increased the responsibility of the Belgian Commander-in-Chief. To the general public, it sounded as if the Allies, following their generous impulse, had rushed to the rescue of the small country victim of German aggression, assuming greater risks and exposing themselves to greater danger in order to safeguard Belgian territory.

As a matter of fact, the reciprocal obligations of Belgium, France and Great Britain, had been very clearly defined by the so-called "Declaration" published in 1937, after the denunciation of the Treaty of Locarno by Germany and the reoccupation of the Rhineland. Belgium had waited six months, from March to October 1936, in the hope that some new Western Pact might be concluded. This hope was not realized, and the international situation deteriorated more and more, mainly owing to the Spanish Civil War. Under Locarno, Belgium was bound not only to defend her own frontiers, but also to defend the frontiers of France who had recently concluded a military pact with Soviet Russia, and had other commitments in Central Europe, notably in Czecho-Slovakia. In March 1936, the four remaining Locarno Powers, namely, Great Britain, France, Italy and Belgium, had decided to keep in close touch and to initiate conversations between General Staffs. This was obviously a temporary arrangement, pending the conclusion of the new pact which was supposed to insure the peace of Europe. Under pressure of public opinion, the Belgian Government asked Great Britain and France to release their country from her commitments under Locarno. This, the two Powers agreed to do in their joint Declaration of April 1937, on condition that Belgium should take all necessary measures to strengthen her defences and prevent another Power from using her territory as a military base. They also maintained their guarantee given under Locarno, i.e., their promise to give Belgium every assistance in case of attack, a guarantee similar to that given in 1839 by the European Powers in the treaty popularly known as the "scrap of paper".[1]

Without in the least minimizing the generosity which prompted Great Britain and France to consent to this change in the international status of Belgium, it should be noted that diplomatic conventions are not concluded on the spur of the moment and are not merely prompted by disinterested motives. The Declaration suited Great Britain and France because, as it will be explained later, it provided at the time the best means of improving the military position of Belgium, an essential factor of European security.

The "anguished appeal" mentioned by M. Reynaud was therefore the automatic result of the invasion of Belgian territory. King Leopold "appealed" to the guarantor Powers in 1940 as King Albert had appealed to them in 1914. He notified them that Belgian terri-

[1] See also p. 96.

4

tory had been violated, that he intended to defend it, according to his international obligations and that he trusted they would do the same, according to theirs. He behaved like the civilized head of a civilized nation appealing to other civilized nations. Hitler had also, in 1937, given a solemn undertaking not to violate Belgian territory and even to defend it if it were to be violated by others, but the Reich never considered itself bound morally or legally by international obligations in the conduct of war.

It is, no doubt, to this German Declaration, confirmed in August, 1939, that M. Reynaud referred when he mentioned that, until May 10th, King Leopold "always affected to attach as much worth to Germany's word as to that of the Allies." This statement is remarkable coming from a lawyer. Either the French Premier had lost all knowledge of diplomatic history or he wished to create the impression that the King, having always had pro-German leanings, had chosen this opportunity of deserting the Allies. Hitler, it must be remembered, had spontaneously offered to guarantee Belgian territory in 1936. The fact that the Belgian Government accepted this offer at a time when both France and Great Britain were still hoping to conclude a treaty with the Reich, and nearly a year before Munich, is not sufficient evidence to show that King Leopold did not make any distinction between Allied and Nazi morality.

2. *Neutrality and the Offensive*

M. Reynaud had from the first chafed against the refusal of Belgium to commit herself and to depart from the neutral attitude she had taken in September 1939, and which was the unavoidable consequence of the position she had occupied since April 1937. For him, to be neutral was to "attach as much worth to Germany's word as to that of the Allies". He tried on more than one occasion to alter this attitude. "Since he had become Premier and promised to conduct the war 'with increased vigour'," writes André Maurois, "he felt obliged to undertake large projects. He reopened the question of Belgium. Was it necessary to wait for an appeal from the Belgian Government before entering Belgium? Reynaud tried to force the Belgians' hand: 'Are you with us or against us?' he asked the Belgian Minister. 'If you are with us, then let us hasten to co-operate in strengthening the defences of our frontiers. If you are against us ——.' " Politics influenced strategy and strategy, in its turn, affected the Premier's conception of international law. He might have spoken in the same way to the Dutch or the Norwegians if they had occupied the same position on the map. He singled out the Belgians because they barred the road to the Rhineland and to the Ruhr, to the weakest link in the Siegfried Line.

During the first months of the war similar demands had already been made, but they had not been so pressing, no doubt because M. Daladier shared General Gamelin's views that " in this war the first one who comes out of his shell will be in great danger." As long as France remained on the defensive, Belgian armed neutrality suited her plans. The presence of 500,000 to 600,000 men on the Belgo-German frontier and the construction of defensive works in Belgian territory operated as a screen behind which she was able to organize her own defences. If it could not stop the *Blitz*, it could at least delay it and prevent a surprise attack.[1]

This defensive policy has been denounced since as having paralyzed the Allies' initiative and demoralized the French army. It is difficult, however, to imagine, in the light of the events of May–June 1940, what other course the Generalissimo could have followed. Superior equipment in the air and on land gave the Germans an enormous advantage as soon as the static war became a war of movement. There are good reasons to believe that the blow was timed in order to take full advantage of M. Reynaud's aggressive disposition. If General Gamelin may be criticized, it is not for adopting the defensive, but for taking the responsibility of departing from it for political motives.

Without entering into this controversy, it is important to point out that, as long as Belgian neutrality suited French strategy, it was generally accepted. Objections only arose when the screen against the German offensive in 1939, became an obstacle against the

---

[1] It should be remembered that, in September 1939, France had only 50 divisions in the field and that there were only 3 British divisions in France. After the Polish war, Germany was able to place from 50 to 70 divisions on the Dutch and Belgian frontiers alone.

The service rendered by the Belgian Army, as a covering force, was emphasized, at the time, by several French and British military experts, notably by General Sir Edmund Ironside.

7

Allies' offensive contemplated in 1940. International law was preserved, but its prestige was seriously affected by the new military plans. That it was nevertheless scrupulously respected by the Allies will be a source of comfort to all those who consider that war is not a sufficient excuse for violating legal and moral principles in defence of which it is waged. It is scarcely necessary to add that such a breach would have proved still more disastrous than the strategy and policy pursued in May 1940.

3. *Answering the Appeal*

Another suggestion which runs through M. Reynaud's speech and which was fully developed by its commentators was that, in order to answer King Leopold's appeal, the Allies took risks which they would not have taken if they had not relied on the Belgians' loyalty and on their ability to take their full share of the forthcoming operations.

"To that appeal we responded," said M. Reynaud, "following a plan conceived by the Allied General Staffs last December."

The date is important. The plan of operations through Belgian and Dutch territory was not "improvised" in answer to the appeal, as wrongly stated in *The Times* on May 29th. It had been prepared four months before. French and British troops had for a long time been stationed on the semi-fortified line running along the Belgian frontier, ready to take the offensive. We know that M. Reynaud was eager to seize the first opportunity of converting this project

into a stern reality and to launch an attack which
would have brought the Allies within a few days as
far as Maastricht in the East and Rotterdam in the
North. The plan failed because, according to M.
Reynaud's own declaration before the Senate, on May
22nd, necessary precautions had not been taken by the
French to protect the hinge around which the turning
movement operated. Owing to "incredible mistakes"
the front was broken through at Sedan, and the enemy
Panzer divisions were allowed to proceed to Calais.
The plan ended in disaster not only because, according
to Mr. Churchill's speech of June 18th, the order to
retire given to the Armies of the North was unduly
delayed, but also because these armies had advanced
too fast and too far and could not withdraw from the
position they occupied before the German gap had
been enlarged and consolidated.

It is sometimes contended that, if they went so far it
was in order to support the Belgians who wished
naturally to protect their own territory against invasion. Therefore, runs the argument, the Belgians
must be held responsible not only for their own
failure to hold on to the end, but also for the plan
which the Allied Staffs had prepared in order to help
them.

Why a similar reproach was never addressed to the
Norwegians who were unable to prolong their resistance, in spite of Allied help, or to the Dutch who were
compelled to surrender on May 15th, has never been
explained.

M. Reynaud could not very well accuse King
Leopold of inducing the Allies to modify their plans in

order to support his own effort, and reproach him, at the same time, for not collaborating in the preparation of these plans before the invasion had actually taken place. But, in his eagerness to shift on other shoulders the heavy responsibility for this ill-conceived offensive, he suggested that it was prepared and undertaken mainly to support the Belgian resistance.

From the military point of view, the position of Belgium towards the Powers who had given her a guarantee was exactly the same in 1940 as in 1914. Belgium promised to defend herself to the utmost if she were invaded. The Allies promised to support her to the utmost. In August 1914, the French advance-guard never reached the line of the Dyle which was held by King Albert for a fortnight, before he was compelled to retire on Antwerp. The Allies were unable to go further than Namur, Charleroi and Mons, before their great retreat upon the Marne. It was not before October 3rd, two months after the invasion, that, owing to Mr. Churchill's initiative, British marines co-operated in the defence of Antwerp. Apart from a brigade of French marines reinforcing the Belgians at Dixmude, it was not before October 23rd that a French force appeared on the Yser front. King Albert was subjected to some criticism for not having done the impossible, but he never reproached the Allies for leaving him in the lurch either on the Dyle or even at Antwerp. On the contrary, he approved General Joffre's defensive strategy and foresaw that it would place the enemy in an impossible situation on the Marne. France and Great Britain had fulfilled their obligations as he had fulfilled his. Both sides had done their utmost. *A l'impossible nul n'est tenu.*

If, this time, the Allies were bound by the guarantee of 1937 to support the Belgians, they were not bound to support them exactly in the way they did. Had they been accurately informed of the forces opposed to them —forces superior in equipment if not in numbers—and had they considered that their best plan was to proceed only as far as the Meuse and Louvain, for instance, no one would have had any right to reproach them for not doing more. However anxious the Belgians may have been to protect their whole territory, they would have accepted the inevitable if they had realized the fatal consequences of the Allied advance. From their point of view, nothing could have been more disastrous than what actually happened, a prolonged struggle on Belgian soil, renewing the destructions of 1914, and the complete defeat of France, which would prevent her from giving further assistance to Britain and her Allies, and might even compel her to turn against them.

King Leopold was repeatedly blamed, before and after May 10th, for refusing to come to an understanding with the French in view of combining military efforts. The fact that he and his Ministers considered such an understanding as a breach of neutrality was interpreted as betraying pro-German or anti-French tendencies. It is indeed difficult to reconcile these criticisms with the suggestion that the plan of the Allied offensive had been specially prepared in order to conform with his wishes.[1]

Here again, we have a precedent, for in this matter

[1] For further details, see p. 131.

11

King Leopold followed the example given him by his father, twenty-five years before. The reports published in the French and British "Documents," after the last war, show that the Allies suspected the intentions of the Belgian Government, especially after the failure of Lieut.-Colonel (later General) Bridges, British Military Attaché in Brussels, to initiate "military conversations," in April, 1912. The letters sent to his Government by M. Klobukowski, the French Minister in Brussels, after that date, show an extraordinary ignorance of the rights and duties of neutrals as established by international law, and a strange bias against a Government which was described as sitting on the fence, ready to jump off on the winning side. On the principle that "he that is not with us is against us," any sign of impartiality was interpreted as betraying "malevolent neutrality," if not worse. So strongly was M. Klobukowski influenced by this prejudice that when, on August 3rd, a representative of the Ministry for Foreign Affairs brought him the Belgian answer to the German ultimatum, he greeted him with these words: "Well, you are giving way?"

It was most fortunate, not only for Belgium but for the Allied cause that, in 1940, the Belgians found in Lord Halifax a statesman as fully aware of the cardinal importance of international obligations as his predecessor at the Foreign Office, Lord (then Sir Edward) Grey. The temptation to exert pressure upon Belgium was greater than it had been in 1912–1914, owing to recent events in Denmark and Norway. The rule of law prevailed, but this did not prevent French publicists from launching a campaign against King

Leopold's "neutralism" which prepared the ground for M. Reynaud's attack. Neither did it prevent von Ribbentrop from justifying the crime of May 10th by accusing Belgium of having done what she was bitterly reproached in some Allied quarters for not doing.

4. *The Base of Dunkirk*

The most striking attack made by M. Reynaud against King Leopold is the least excusable, because as head of the French Government he must have had a sufficient knowledge of the situation in which the Northern Armies were placed not to be waylaid into misrepresenting it.

After pointing out that the Allied armies were divided into two groups, the one stationed on the Somme-Aisne front, the other operating in Flanders and Northern France, he added: "This group of three armies (British, Belgian and French), under the command of General Blanchard, was supplied *via* Dunkirk. The French and British armies defended this port in the South and in the East, and the Belgian army in the North. It is this Belgian army which, at the height of the battle, has unconditionally and without warning its British and French comrades-in-arms, suddenly capitulated on the orders of its King, and opened the road to Dunkirk to the German divisions. . . . King Leopold, without warning General Blanchard, without one thought, without one word for the British and French soldiers who came to the help of his country . . . laid down his arms. It is a fact without precedent in history."

This revelation came at a time when French and British opinion, on the strength of over-optimistic communiqués, still believed that the gap between the Allies might be bridged and that the armies in the North, although sorely pressed, were perfectly able to hold their own. The way military news was "cooked" at the time by the French Press Bureau for home and foreign consumption has been thoroughly exposed by M. Alexander Werth and others. As late as May 24th, the French military spokesman expressed his conviction that the battle engaged "between Valenciennes, Cambrai and Arras" would "continue several days before any definite result could be announced." In the North, the British were "carrying out a withdrawal in orderly fashion without being pressed by the enemy." The breach between the Allied forces north of the Somme was only "twenty-five miles wide." "The enemy reinforcements which were sent through were being harassed by Allied artillery and the roads were constantly bombed."

Read in connection with the news published on the previous days, the impression given by M. Reynaud's speech was that of two powerful groups of armies waging an uncertain but by no means desperate battle from two different bases, while the truth was that the Armies in the North were entirely cut off from their bases which had always been in France. Dunkirk, Nieuport and Ostend were only a makeshift, improvised after the German divisions had reached Abbeville. Owing to the German mastery in the air, these ports were constantly bombed and could not supply the Allies with sufficient food and munitions. The Belgians

14

and, to a lesser degree, the British, had suffered from this shortage during the last days.

In the same way, M. Reynaud's account suggested that, in the event of an Allied success, the famous counter-offensive with which public anxiety had been lulled since General Weygand had succeeded Gamelin, might at last take place, and the two portions of the Allied forces be joined together. We know now—and M. Reynaud must have known then—that all attempts made in that direction had already failed, and that, certainly since the 26th and probably before that date, the British, having given up all hope of "cutting through," had proceeded with their grim preparations for evacuating as many men as possible through Dunkirk, leaving their equipment behind and proceeding with the necessary destructions.[1]

The surrender of the Belgian army did not wreck a counter-offensive which had never been allowed to materialize. Neither did it cause the retreat upon Dunkirk which had started several days before. The accusation is therefore narrowed to this single question: did the Belgians jeopardize this retreat or did they do their utmost to make it possible? This point will be dealt with in a later chapter. For the present, it is enough to confront the French Premier's description of the military operations, with that given by several British military experts during the last months, to show that he was more influenced by the desire of piling up evidence against the man he chose to denounce, than by a keen sense of truth and justice.

[1] See pp. 168, 169.

15

5. *"Without Warning General Blanchard"*

This is apparently accurate, and General Blanchard was "at the head of the three armies," French, Belgian and British, operating in the North. Those who heard this statement were unavoidably led to suspect treachery. Indeed, it would have been impossible for any responsible statesman to express in stronger terms his conviction that the head of a neighbouring State had committed treason.

At a meeting held at Casteau, near Mons, on May 12th, attended by General Gort, General Billotte and King Leopold, the latter, as Commander-in-Chief of the Belgian Army, had agreed that General Billotte, acting under the instruction of General Gamelin, should be placed in supreme command. The unity of command established from the beginning of the war in France, between the French and the British, was thus extended to Belgium. General Billotte had been the victim of a motor accident a week before the capitulation, and Weygand, who had succeeded Gamelin after the débâcle of Sedan, had designated General Blanchard to succeed him. The King was therefore in duty bound to follow General Blanchard's instructions and not to take any important decision without consulting him, or if consultation were impossible, without warning him. And he had not warned him. At least General Blanchard could in all sincerity declare to M. Reynaud that "he had received no warning."

Before being a politician, M. Reynaud had been a distinguished barrister, and as a barrister he knew how to handle evidence. The fact that the only French superior officer connected with these events who had not been warned happened to be the one who was entitled by his position to expect the warning, suited M. Reynaud admirably. He could not say that the French and British Missions at Belgian Headquarters had not been kept informed of the plight in which the Belgian troops found themselves, of the danger of capitulation unless some measure of support reached them before it was too late, or of the King's decision to act at last in order to avoid a useless massacre or a dangerous rout; he could not express himself in this way without exposing himself to a flat contradiction as soon as the facts were made known. But he could very safely say that "General Blanchard" had not been advised of the King's decision, because the Chief of the French Mission at Belgian Headquarters had not succeeded in communicating with General Blanchard's Headquarters on May 27th, and in transmitting to him the message he had received from the King.

From a memorandum of these events drafted at Laeken by the King's advisers, on June 3rd, and from other sources, we learn that, on the 26th, at noon, General Champon, the Head of the French Mission, received a note containing the following words: "The Belgian Command asks you to make it known to the Generalissimo of the Allied Armies that the situation of the Belgian Army is critical (*grave*) and that the Commander-in-Chief intends to pursue the struggle *until the complete exhaustion of the means at his disposal.* . . . The enemy is attacking from Eecloo to Menin.

17   C

The limit of resistance is very nearly reached."[1] This message remained unanswered.

At 6 p.m. General Blanchard called at Belgian Headquarters. He announced that the British were evacuating their positions on the frontier (on the right of the Belgian Army) in order to occupy new positions on a line extending from Lille to Ypres. The French general added that he would only be able to place one mechanized division, reduced to fifteen tanks, in the gap created by this withdrawal. He had not been able to join General Gort and could give no information as to his intentions.

On the 27th, in the morning, the King heard that the Belgian front had been broken in several places, particularly in the centre. All his reserves had been used up. He telegraphed to General Gort at 12.30 that "the morale of his troops was very shaken (*très découragé*) after four days' ceaseless fighting under an intense bombardment which the R.A.F. was unable to prevent. The knowledge that the Allied armies were surrounded and that the enemy possessed a great superiority in the air had led his men to believe that their position was desperate. The moment was rapidly nearing when they would be unable to pursue the fight. *The King will be compelled to capitulate in order to avoid a rout.*"

In the afternoon, King Leopold summoned a meeting of the members of his General Staff. They unanimously agreed at 4 p.m. that from the international as well as from the national point of view, capitulation was the only means of avoiding a worse disaster caused

[1] The italics are mine.—A.

18

by an abortive attempt to pursue the retreat in a strip of territory congested with Allied troops and civilians. It was decided that a *parlementaire* should be sent to German Headquarters to enquire on what conditions hostilities could be brought to an end.

Some time before, about 2.30 p.m., General Weygand's *Aide Major-Général*, who happened to be at Belgian Headquarters, had been told that "Belgian resistance was practically at an end" and that "the front was breaking". The decision to capitulate was immediately communicated to the Chiefs of the British and French Missions, and to Admiral Sir Roger Keyes. General Champon, while acknowledging its necessity, expressed the opinion that negotiations should be conducted jointly by the Commander-in-Chiefs of the three armies. *He said that "he had succeeded in communicating with General Weygand by wireless, but that he had failed to reach General Blanchard whose headquarters were no longer in the same position".* The same difficulty impeded communications with General Gort who had been unable to establish himself in Cassel and who could not be reached by telephone, owing to the destruction of the *Centrale* at Lille.[1]

General Weygand's answer was received on the 28th at 3.15 a.m., five hours before M. Reynaud made his speech. It is scarcely believable that when the Generalissimo communicated the news of the Belgian capitulation to the French Premier, he did not inform him at the same time of the way it had reached him, and of the previous emphatic warnings he had received

[1] But a wireless message to British G.H.Q. and a telegram to the War Office were at once dispatched by the British Mission.

19

from Belgian Headquarters. Besides, the members of the Belgian Cabinet, who had had a dramatic interview with their Sovereign on the 25th, during which the possibility of surrender had been mentioned as well as the King's intention to remain with his army if the worst came to the worst, had seen M. Reynaud, on the 26th and 27th, and described to him the desperate straits in which the Belgian Army was placed, and the state of exhaustion reached by the divisions which were still able to withstand the enemy's relentless assaults.[1] Aware that the Allies were themselves hard pressed and unable to send any reinforcements, the French Premier could entertain no illusions as to the ultimate issue of the battle. He also knew that the King had refused to leave Belgium. His surprise was therefore feigned. It was one of these *effets oratoires* which may be justified when used in order to save the life of a client in a criminal court, but which are less excusable when used by a responsible statesman in order to ruin the reputation of the friendly Sovereign of a friendly state.

For M. Reynaud knew the facts which he distorted or misinterpreted. He was in constant touch with Weygand who, for several days, had decided to cut his losses in the North and to concentrate the defence of France on the Somme-Aisne front. M. Reynaud knew that Dunkirk was no longer a military base from which

[1] The Ministers met M. Reynaud in London, after leaving Belgium. They flew back with him to Paris. On the 27th M. Pierlot, General Denis (Minister of National Defence) and M. Letellier (Belgian Ambassador in Paris) were received by the French Prime Minister. Both Marshal Pétain and General Weygand were present at this interview.

20

operations could be started, but the last port through which a part—it was thought at the time, only a small part—of the Northern Armies could be evacuated, in order to escape capture. He knew that the Belgian Army had since the 24th resisted desperately the onslaught of the enemy, concentrated upon the northern sector of the Allied front, and that this army without supplies, without protection from the air, had reached the limit of physical and moral endurance. He knew that capitulation was unavoidable unless fresh reinforcements could be sent and that these reinforcements could not be sent. He knew that King Leopold, contrary to the advice of his Ministers, intended to remain with his troops if he were obliged to lay down his arms. He knew more than that. According to André Maurois' evidence, he realized already that the French would have as little chance of resisting on the Somme and the Aisne as they had had on the Meuse. On the previous occasion, he had chosen his scapegoats, General Corap and fifteen of his colleagues, not to mention Gamelin. This time, he had no hesitation in choosing another, Leopold, King of the Belgians.

The most favourable interpretation of his indictment has already been given above: "What matter the reputation of a single man if France be saved." But we cannot entirely dismiss a less favourable interpretation: "What matter King Leopold's reputation if M. Reynaud's can be saved." History will perhaps conclude that, at this moment, the French Premier identified his own fate with that of his country.

6. *"Without one thought, without one word . . ."*

The advocate turned prosecuting counsel enlarged upon King Leopold's responsibility towards the Allies. Not only did the King give no warning, but he gave no excuse. He was apparently so anxious to save his crown or his life that he gave up the struggle when the fate of the Northern Armies hung in the balance, "at the height of the battle", without apologizing in any way for his action, without making any provision in order to safeguard his comrades-in-arms from its fatal consequences.

M. Reynaud could have no knowledge, on May 28th, of the letter written, on the same day, from Bruges, by the King to the Pope and to President Roosevelt. If it had been published at the time the French and British public might at least have heard that the accused pleaded "Not guilty": "Amid the general confusion provoked by the stupendous events through which we are living and which succeed each other so rapidly, I wish to declare that Belgium and her army have done all their duty. Belgium has kept her international obligations, first in maintaining a scrupulous neutrality, later in defending inch by inch her whole territory." After describing the way in which the Belgians had been obliged to retire from their strong positions in front of Brussels owing to "military events which occurred outside Belgian territory", the Commander-in-Chief added: "Our army has spent itself without stint during a four days' battle (May 24th–28th) waged in co-operation with the Allied armies. We found ourselves at last encircled, on a small strip of territory, with a dense population greatly increased by hundreds of thousands of refugees without shelter, without food, without drinking water, and driven hither and thither by aerial bombardment. Yesterday, our last means of resistance were broken under the weight of the enemy's crushing superiority on land and in the air. In these circumstances, I tried to avoid the prolongation of a struggle which would have led to our extermination without profit for the Allies. No one has the right to sacrifice human lives uselessly."

These were "the real facts" (*la réalité des faits*), very different from the interpretation the French Premier had given them a few hours before. The accused may have been heard by the Pope and by the American President. Owing to the censorship or for other reasons he was heard by no one else. It was not a proper trial and, according to judicial practice, the right of appeal must be granted.

Those were the King's words at the time. What were his actions?

At a meeting held at Ypres, on May 21st, at which General Weygand explained the plan of his counter-offensive to the Chiefs of the Allied armies in the North, King Leopold had undertaken to extend his front on the Lys as far as Menin, in order to cover the Franco-British attack, from the South and from the North, in the region of Albert and Arras. His depleted divisions, weakened by a painful and difficult retreat were to hold a line 56 miles long upon which fresh German troops supported by air bombardment and tanks, concentrated their attack. In order to stiffen his soldiers' efforts, in his order of the day of May 25th, he urged them to "resist to the end" and promised them, whatever happened, to "share their fate".

He had a twofold duty to fulfil. His national duty was to defend Belgian territory, his international duty, to co-operate loyally with the guarantor Powers who had answered his appeal.

This twofold duty was not forgotten when capitulation was discussed at the meeting of the Belgian Staff held on the 27th. Here is an extract of the minutes of this meeting according to the Laeken memorandum. The Belgian Command agreed:

(1) "that, from the national standpoint, the national army fulfilled its task by exerting all its power and exhausting all its means of resistance (*la totalité de sa capacité de résistance*). Its units would be incapable of resuming the struggle, on the morrow. Further retirement on the Yser cannot be contemplated. It would disintegrate the units more than fighting. It would increase still further the congestion of the Allied forces dangerously packed together between the Yser, on the one side, Calais and Cassel—already attacked by the Germans —on the other.

(2) "that, from the international point of view, the sending of a *parlementaire* to enquire about the conditions of a suspension of hostilities would give the Allies a respite during the night of May 27th–28th and a few hours the next morning, a respite which could only be obtained, by pursuing the fight, at the cost of a complete dislocation (*dislocation catastrophique*) of the Army."

In other words, from the Allied point of view, and

especially from the point of view of the evacuation from Dunkirk, the consequences of surrender were not so dangerous as the consequences of a complete rout.

All this M. Reynaud should have known, since the reasons for the decision had been made plain to General Champon and since the latter communicated with the Generalissimo and received his answer. But public indignation had to be whipped into white fury, and neither General Champon nor General Weygand were likely to speak. The only allied officer who uttered a word of protest was Sir Roger Keyes who, as Special Liaison Officer with King Leopold was also informed of these proceedings and who, on his return to England, warned his compatriots not to judge rashly "a very gallant soldier".[1]

There are other facts which show that, far from ignoring the Allies' interests, King Leopold took every precaution to safeguard them. On May 27th, some British technicians, attached to the Belgian Air Force, were told of the impending decision and left the Front with all their equipment. The same day, the French 60th Division, which had co-operated with the Belgians after its retreat from Holland, was sent to the coast in Belgian lorries and placed along the Yser on positions previously prepared by the Belgian Army. These arrangements were made by mutual agreement with General Champon, and at his request. Of this, once more, both General Weygand and M. Reynaud must have been informed.

[1] See Preface. I wish to state that all the information given in this chapter and in chapters VI and VII is derived from Belgian sources, and was set down before I had any opportunity of meeting Sir Roger Keyes after his return from Belgium.

7. *"Against his responsible Ministers"*

"The Belgian Government informed me that the King's decision was taken against the unanimous feeling of his responsible Ministers."

There is in this statement the same mixture of truth and untruth which characterizes the speech from beginning to end. "General Blanchard" had received no warning, but everyone else had. The King and his Ministers disagreed about something, therefore they disagreed about everything.

When the Belgian Ministers met the French Premier, on the 26th and 27th, they told him that the object of their visit to Belgian Headquarters two days before, had been to persuade their Sovereign to leave Belgium, as Queen Wilhelmina had left Holland, and as King Haakon had left Norway. There had indeed been a clash between their interpretation and King Leopold's interpretation of the Sovereign's duties and responsibilities under the Constitution. They considered him above all as Head of the State, he considered himself above all as Head of the Army. The Sovereign and his Ministers frankly disagreed on this question and their last interview was certainly a painful one, but neither the King nor his Ministers presumed to dictate to each other the policy they should follow in their own sphere of activity. M. Pierlot could not decide whether and when capitulation had become necessary. King Leopold, on the other hand, by remaining in Belgium under enemy occupation, soon realised that he could no longer exercise his power as Head of the Executive. The main difference between them was not whether the Army should have surrendered when it did, but whether, after this surrender, or shortly before it, the Sovereign should relinquish his command and resume the position which he occupied before the invasion.

This plain truth was once more twisted in order to isolate the accused, and to suggest that he had been decisively and definitely disowned by his most responsible collaborators.[1]

8. *"A fact without precedent"*

What was without precedent? The capitulation of an army before the enemy? Without ransacking the pages of history, the French Premier might have been referred to the capitulation of Metz, and to the first Battle of Sedan in 1870. More recently, he might have been reminded of the Norwegian capitulation, and of the Dutch capitulation. He emphasized the fact that it had been "unconditional". Did he consider an armistice such as the one which ended the last war in 1918, or which was soon to end the battle of France, more honourable than an unconditional surrender? Is it more concordant with military honour to give up the fight when you have still something left to bargain with, or when you have exhausted all resources in a loyal effort to defend yourself in an unequal battle, and are literally left at the mercy of your enemy?

King Leopold's action was not without precedent, but M. Reynaud's certainly was. It would be impossible to find in history, or at any rate in modern history, an

[1] See also p. 172.

27

indictment of the Head of an allied and friendly nation, made by the leader of another allied and friendly nation more inaccurate and more biased than this speech of May 28th. There is not a sentence in it —or at least in the part concerned with King Leopold —which is not either incorrect or warped by passion and prejudice.

Without taking into account the recent criticisms made against M. Reynaud's private and public life, and judging every point of the speech on its merits, as if it had been delivered by the most trustworthy statesman whose conduct had hitherto been devoid of ambition and self-interest, it stands as a terrible indictment, not against King Leopold, but against its author.

I have devoted some space to it, not merely because I wish to dispel the evil influence it has had on the reputation of my King and of my country, but also because it is the root of the legend which has grown ever since and which, in spite of the publication of conclusive evidence, has not yet been completely eradicated.

There are good and evil legends, legends which adorn a noble truth, and legends which adorn an ignoble untruth. The more this untruth is deliberate the more ignoble it becomes. I have tried to reduce the deliberate character of M. Reynaud's false statements as much as possible, and trust that, when his evidence can be heard, he will be able to reduce it still further.

One thing should be added. I said that the influence of the indictment was increased by the prestige which France enjoyed at the time, but I do not mean to suggest that France was responsible for it, even if she endorsed it. France, Britain and the United States were to a great extent convinced by the denunciation because they trusted M. Reynaud or because they believed that no statesman in his position could speak as he spoke if he were not sure of his facts, if he did not know even more than he revealed. A great number of Belgians, particularly among the refugees, shared this view. The indictment was made by one man; the legend created by the indictment spread everywhere. France is no more responsible for it than any other country. On the contrary, it was the legitimate reputation she enjoyed as the defender of truth and justice which added still more weight to her leader's words.

Chapter II

REMINISCENCES

1. *Comparing Notes*

TWO DAYS AFTER M. Reynaud's speech, I called on
my friend L., a Belgian who had, like myself, spent
most of his life in England. As I entered the room, I
ran into a well-known British publicist who met me
with a sad smile. He looked as if he had just attended
a funeral.

I found L. scowling angrily.

"Do you know what he told me," he broke out as
soon as he had recovered his temper. "We should disown the King. Even if he does not abdicate, he will
never be able to show his face again. No one will
follow him, neither the Government, nor the Army,
nor the people. As for the Allies, how can they ever
reinstate him on his throne in the event of victory?
We should apparently cut our losses, like Weygand,
turn to the future, forget the past, let bygones be bygones and concentrate our whole strength on fresh
preparations. This royal controversy is a dead weight
which will drag us down if we do not drop it at once
and for ever."

"Fortunately, it does not depend on us," I remarked.

"Nevertheless, every Belgian has his duty to fulfil.
We must serve the country, what is left of it, as well as
we can. We must shoulder our responsibilities."

"We agree," I said, "that the King is no longer able
to exercise his power. As long as he is in the enemy's

hands, we must obey our Government's instructions."

"The conflict between the Sovereign and his Government is purely constitutional. It may be the result of a misunderstanding. It may be cleared up. But the conflict between the Commander-in-Chief of the Belgian Army and the leaders of Britain and France is a much graver matter. You have heard Reynaud's speech; you have read the papers, what are you going to do?"

"Wait for further information."

"Wait, when the storm is let loose, when every hour piles up more abuse, more infamy! It is not the King's reputation only which is at stake, it is that of the whole country. We are all in it. This is not Republican France, this is England and, in England, King and country are one. Reynaud's speech was bad enough. The comments are worse."

"The solution proposed by your friend is the easiest way out. He believes that the wisest course is to choose . . ."

"But I do not choose to choose," shouted L., banging his fist on the table.

"Neither do I."

"Why?"

"Because I am not satisfied with Reynaud's statement."

"But how can we contradict it? The facts are plain enough. The Army, we are told, was full of fight. It had, during the last days succeeded in repulsing the enemy on several occasions. It was co-operating with the British and the French. Anything might still have happened. Reinforcements might have been sent from this country. The Allies might have fought on two fronts until the Germans, worn out by their huge effort, had paid the penalty for their bold advance as they did on the Marne. And it is just that crucial moment, without warning, without a word, for no apparent reason, that the King chooses to surrender. I was prepared for anything, for invasion, for defeat, but not for that."

"Yes," I added, "and there are innuendos. Why did he refuse to come here, like King Haakon and Queen Wilhelmina? Why did he choose to stay behind, as if he did not wish Belgium to fight on? What are the conditions of the capitulation? What does he hope to do. If he does nothing, his sacrifice is useless; if he acts, whence will he derive his authority? From Hitler?"

"Don't," protested L.

"We don't believe Reynaud, we two and a handful of others. But everyone does—implicitly. They think they know the answer and they certainly don't know the accused. There must be an explanation. Our first duty is to try and stop this. Is there any way to find out?"

"Can't you imagine I have tried? I have pestered the Embassy until they are sick of the sight of me. They have no news to give me. They can still communicate with Paris, but all I can get from them is M. Pierlot's speech. It all boils down to this, the Sovereign has lost all power and the Government pursues the struggle. This is no explanation. What we want is facts, facts about our losses, about the state of the Army at the time, about supplies, about the progress of the enemy, about the exact situation occupied, on the 27th, by the French, British and Belgian armies, about the resources of Dunkirk."

"And there would still remain," I added, "the mystery of withholding information from Blanchard and of the decision to remain behind."

"Meanwhile, our demoralized refugees are pouring into London. Belgian reputation is going to the dogs, the King is trampled in the mud in scores of articles and cartoons. You are too patient!"

"I am patient because I am confident. Either we are wrong, and then all is over, or we are right, and the storm will pass. I have faith not only in Belgian honesty but in the British sense of justice."

"The British don't know the King as we do."

"Very well, then, let us compare notes. Let us explore together his antecedents."

"An ugly word."

"Why? Antecedents carry a great weight in the judgment of human affairs. When you know a man well, you are reluctant to accept a damning accusation made against him. Your first movement is an emphatic denial. When, however, the accusation is made by someone whom you have no reason to distrust, your second movement is to revive your own memories and go carefully over the whole ground, from the beginning of this man's career to his last action, and examine how far that action, as it is interpreted, tallies with your own evidence or contradicts it."

"You are very cool about it. You forget that we are talking of our King."

"I am not forgetting it, but in present circum-

stances, the King is a man like you and me, and no
man is above certain temptations. Let us therefore dismiss, for the present, all idea of blind loyalty and respect. Let us open our eyes and scrutinize the past.
Nothing is impossible, but some things are so im-
probable that they may be considered as impossible.
I have still to learn that a stream which runs clear for
many miles becomes suddenly muddy without a
plausible motive. I have still to learn that a man who
has led from his early boyhood a clean and unimpeachable life can, on the spur of the moment, lose
all dignity and honour, and that his candid frankness
can be turned into treacherous duplicity. This is our
problem and, since we can do nothing better, we
might do worse than try to solve it."

"As you wish."

So we lit our pipes, mixed another drink, and, after
lifting our glasses in a silent toast to our much
maligned monarch, we began to compare notes. L.
had more to say about Prince Leopold's youth, having
served through the last war and having had several
friends among the members of King Albert's household. I had more to say about King Leopold's life and
policy in recent years. A verbatim record of our
rambling talk, which frequently wandered from the
straight path of chronological order, would appear
somewhat confusing. Certain pictures, however,
passed before our eyes during that evening in the
vivid light of our bitter grief, things which we had
seen, others which had been described to us by some
eye-witness. Some of them were cruel, others com-

forting. They all point to the same conclusion. I shall try to reproduce them as well as I can.

2. *La Panne*, 1915

A blustery April day, on the sandy shore of the fishing village and seaside resort of La Panne, the last refuge of King Albert and his family, behind the front. A square of soldiers wearing the old blue uniform and *képi* of a regiment of the line—the glorious XIIth, well-known for its desperate counter-attacks through the marshy meadows along the Yser, now covered by the protecting flood. In the midst of the square, a tall officer, the King, talking to his men. In front of him, standing to attention, a tall, slender boy in the uniform of a private.

A strong wind is blowing. Only snatches of the speech can be heard by a few spectators, among them Lord Athlone and Princess Alice: . . . "Princes must be brought up in the school of duty. . . . My son has claimed the honour of wearing the uniform of our valiant soldiers . . ."

The Prince looks very frail, in a greatcoat cut too long for him, but the men detect a strange determination in his boyish face. He is only 13. Never before did a boy of that age volunteer as a private in a modern army. Never did a Royal Prince serve in the ranks. How would he stand life in the trenches, the constant shelling, the drudgery work of filling sacks and incessantly rebuilding the crumbling parapet, the sleepless nights, the close atmosphere of the shelters? Bad enough for men, not good enough for a boy brought up in luxury and comfort. This, they thought,

35

was just what "Albert" would do. He did not spare himself. He allowed the Queen to take risks, visiting them at the front. It was his way of doing things.

The Colonel of the XIIth did not relish the fresh responsibility entrusted him by his Chief. He liked it still less when the latter took him apart, telling him that Leopold should work like the others: "Make him dig in the trenches so that he shall know what it is to have blistered hands."

The happiest person in that square was Leopold himself. He was not needed at home. Let his younger brother Charles and his sister Marie-José accompany their mother on her rounds, in the hospitals and the schools of the district. He was no longer a child. He wished to take his share of his father's work. Discipline for discipline, he preferred the time-table of the army to the time-table of the class-room. He had remained behind too long, in Brussels, in Antwerp, in Lord Curzon's house in England, and at last here, in La Panne, in the small villa where they all lived together. He wished to go to the front, and since he had been brought up in the hard school of princes, as his father understood it, he "claimed the privilege" to go to the hard school of war.

The wind blew through the reeds in the sand-dunes and swept the shore. The tide was rising. As the glorious XIIth filed past the Commander-in-Chief, Prince Leopold who had taken his place in the ranks, walking in step with his new comrades, saluted his father with a proud heart.

3.   *Eton*, 1916

Fourteen months later. A tall boy in an Eton suit,

sitting at his desk in his study. He seems to have some difficulty in concentrating on his task, an English essay. From time to time, Leopold looks through the open window towards the distant trees and the drifting clouds. He came here eight months ago, soon after Dr. Lyttleton, the Headmaster, had paid a short visit to La Panne. That was his father's idea. He had been made to understand that he could not go on serving in the army for years. A future King must be an educated man and, since England had excellent schools, he should go to an English school. This would be an opportunity of practising his English and becoming a true sportsman. It was all so plausible that he could raise no objection. His father was always plausible. No doubt he was right too, but it was hard to be away from it all.

He went to the window. English fields and, against the bright June sky, the deep masses of English elms with their cascade of dark foliage. The winding river in the distance; closer, the brick buildings of the College, and on the playing ground some of the smaller boys in white flannels engaged in a game of cricket. There is a bluish haze over it all, the haze which succeeds a series of rainy days. Some booming noise suggests to Leopold the distant sound of guns. He no longer sees green fields but greyish mud, no longer massive trees but barkless trunks and dead branches mangled by shrapnel, no longer a smiling, winding river but stinking marshes covered with yellow rushes, no longer the proud old square and the noble chapel but wrecked houses and disembowelled churches.

There is peace here and quiet leisure. Provided a certain code is observed, life runs smoothly from hour to hour, from task to task, from match to match. Everything is clean and tidy and composed. He likes things to be clean and tidy. He loves the silence only interrupted by the peal of bells and the shouting of boyish voices. It is certainly better than the din of bombardment, the screaming of shells and the tremor of bombs. Still, in spite of everything, he regrets La Panne and the front, his cheerful mother, his grave father and the grin of his grimy companions. He counts the weeks and the days which bring the holidays closer. Speech-day soon with its top hats, morning suits and spats, pomp and ceremony, bright colours and lovely frocks. Then back to the trenches, while the other fellows go home to drink tea and eat ice creams. . . .

The door creaks. Leopold, roused from his dreams, turns abruptly to see his tutor looking over his half-finished essay.

"Work has been difficult to-day?"

"I am sorry, Sir, I shall do better to-morrow. I was *un peu distrait*. Can one say, absent?"

"Absent-minded?"

"Absent-minded, yes."[1]

[1] The King never forgot the months spent at Eton. On several occasions he invited deputations from the school to visit him in Brussels and remained in close touch with the Master who had been his tutor.

Cf. M. W. Fodor, *The Revolution is On*, p. 79: "Ever since his childhood, the young King had entertained a certain animosity against England . . . partly attributable to his unfortunate experience during his public-school days in England . . ."

4. *The Return*

More than two years later. A cold and bright
November day. The long Rue Royale, in Brussels, is
crowded to the roofs. From the black masses of people
covering the pavements, surging from every window,
comes a constant roar, almost painful in its intensity.
He rides beside his mother, a little behind the King, at
the head of the Belgian troops, behind American,
French and British detachments. He feels terribly excited but does his best to hide it. Self-control has become a discipline with him which the months spent at
Eton have fortified. The Duke of York is there too,
riding on the other side of the Queen. Leopold
watches his father's grave face, while he salutes the
crowd with a sweep of his sword. It is difficult not to
smile, from time to time, looking on these laughing,
exultant faces, the outstretched hands, the waving
handkerchiefs, the children held up above the heads
of their parents. How they cheer, how happy they are!

His horse, excited by the noise, drops into a short
canter and he has some difficulty in bringing him back
in step with the band. The cobblestones are slippery.
There must be no untoward incident. Nothing should
mar the day. For this is the day for which they have
all been waiting, his family in La Panne, the men in
the trenches and these millions of civilians in Belgium, under the yoke of the invader. As soon as
Leopold heard about the great offensive he asked to
come back from Eton. He felt sure that this time the
Allies would sweep everything before them. He had
been there during the tragic days of invasion. It was

39

only fair that he should witness the deliverance. He had missed the surprise visit to Ostend, improvised by Sir Roger Keyes, on the morrow of the enemy's departure, before the Belgian troops had reached the town, but he had taken part in the entry into Bruges, on October 25th, and, a few days later, into Antwerp. He had never thought that such enthusiasm could be surpassed.

Somewhat dazed by the noise, he feels that he is witnessing a scene which he will never forget. He tries to take it all in, not to miss any detail. "I must remember this," he thinks, and, as he does so, he notices, between the houses and the public massed on the pavement, a long file of stretcher-bearers carrying fainting men and women to the nearest Red Cross post. And he realizes what gives such a poignancy to this wild enthusiasm: Many have not enough strength left to stand the strain of so much joy.

This was the day when he promised himself to devote his life wholly to Belgium.

5. *Accession*

February 23rd, 1934. After riding through the town, King Leopold stands bare-headed before deputies and senators, ready to address them on the day of his accession. A week before, the nation had been staggered by the news of King Albert's sudden death from a climbing accident, among the rocks of Marche-les-Dames, on the Meuse. Queen Elisabeth is still almost distracted by the news. She has lost her husband, he has lost his father, counsellor and friend, the wise and strong man whom he trusted above all men and who,

40

for many years to come, should have prepared him to carry the heavy responsibilities which have now so suddenly been placed upon his shoulders.

When pleased with his work or with the reports he gave him of his long journeys to the United States, Brazil, the Sudan, the Congo and the Dutch Indies, his father had told him repeatedly that he was ready to succeed him. Would he show himself worthy of these encouraging words now that he was called upon to fill the place of his great predecessor?

Looking round, he sees, on the raised platform, Queen Astrid between their children, Astrid who, within a few years, has won the heart of all by her simplicity and warm-hearted sympathy. Here is a fresh source of strength which will not fail him. But he will need it all and God's help to overcome the obstacles which lie ahead.

These difficulties crowded around him while he was preparing this speech which he must now deliver. After fifteen years, the country has not yet recovered from the war and the long and cruel foreign occupation. She has risen from her ruins, but she is still involved in financial difficulties, recently aggravated by the world depression. There are divisions in the land which even his father, with all his prestige, did not succeed in reconciling. Clouds are accumulating on the political horizon. Japan has struck a deadly blow at the League, Hitler is in power beyond the Rhine. Great Britain and France, on whose preparedness Belgian security closely depends, seem too much absorbed by their internal affairs to devote much attention to the danger ahead.

He is conscious of a few smiles in the large amphi-
theatre. He must not prolong this hushed silence. He
must break it with resolution, show his metal as he
did at La Panne. His father relied on him. All these
people in the streets who followed him with their
acclamations up to the gates of Parliament rely on
him. Belgium relies on him.

He is speaking now and, as he speaks, his voice
grows more steady and he draws a fresh strength from
the response of his audience. He hears himself talking
of the "constant care and deep virtue" of his "deeply
beloved father" for whom the monarchy implied complete devotion to the public cause, of the Constitution
which he has sworn to obey, of his "absolute conviction" that Belgian institutions are "sufficiently supple"
to adapt themselves to the necessities of the time.
Belgium will "continue to contribute to the organization of peace," while "making all the necessary sacrifices to safeguard her territory and her liberties".

Echoes from another and graver voice? What better
course could he take? The path has been traced by his
guide, he can only follow in his footsteps. The problems are the same, the policy should be the same. It
would be sheer vanity to try and discover any other
way. Then, associating Queen Astrid and his children
with his peroration, he exclaims: "I give myself wholly
to Belgium!"

It is the realization of the promise made fifteen
years ago.[1]

[1] See Appendix I.

6. *Astrid*

"And didn't he keep it, during the six following years," said L. "I remember seeing him a few days after Queen Astrid's funeral, in September '35. He wore his arm in a sling and the wound on his face was not yet healed, but he was already at work. They call him stubborn! You would have to be stubborn to stand such a blow in such a way. They doubt his courage, but they dare not doubt his love for her and for his children.

"After his father's death, he had devoted himself to his task with a conscientiousness and a thoroughness which astonished his Ministers. He insisted on examining everything himself. His part was not to order, but to advise, and he wished to be informed before advising. He was at his desk, on the morrow of King Albert's death. He spent most of the day in his study.

"Before this last tragedy, he took a day off, from time to time at his old home of Stuyvenberg where Queen Astrid and her three children were waiting for him. There were brief moments of relaxation when he could think of something else than financial crises, currency, deflation, extraordinary powers, or the fluctuations of his Ministers' popularity.

"They had been looking forward, this year, to their summer holidays in the Alps. The Queen knew how to enjoy life and to make him share her joy. Everything favoured them; there was a lull in political strife, the financial crisis was almost overcome and the weather seemed settled for a long spell of sunny days. Every morning the Queen saw that the King was

43

recovering something of his old eagerness for climbing, of this deep enthusiasm for nature which he had inherited from his father. He lost that worried look which he had worn since the news of King Albert's death had reached them in February, the year before. He was no longer overwhelmed by his sense of responsibility, and she heard again with delight his old boyish laughter, his father's laughter.

"Well, that drive at Küssnacht put an end to it. He never recovered it even when, weeks later, he played again with the children. Astrid gone, work remained his only passion. Duty, an exacting sense of duty, filled all his life and followed him after he had left the Palace for Laeken. He was and remained a widower. He mourned for the Queen. He mourned for the loss of past hopes and of that sense of security which had already begun to disturb Europe. He was haunted by the presentiment that Belgium might one day share the fate of Astrid and perish also in some terrible catastrophe."

7.   *The Five Last Years*

"Granted," I said, "but from whatever angle I look at it, I cannot discover any word or action of his which reveals discouragement or defeatism. People say now that he could not fight for two weeks, when he had fought incessantly at home and abroad for five years to avoid the catastrophe. They say he lacked energy, when he had shown that the worst tragedies could devastate his life without affecting his strength. He was no escapist, no self-seeker like those to whom he has been compared; his only ambition was to serve his country and prevent her doom. Whether he was right or wrong in the choice of his methods does not concern us now. We are not dealing with political doctrine, but with moral character. Could such a man do such a deed? Was he of the stuff of which traitors are made? His only mistake, if it can be called a mistake, was over-conscientiousness, over-seriousness. As long as Queen Astrid lived, he could relax more easily. Besides, they were one in the eyes of the people and if he looked stern, she walked through life with a perpetual smile on her lips or in her eyes. She helped to bring him in touch with the crowd, to break the ice of the strange shyness which he inherited from his father. When she was gone, he grew still more reserved. Without losing his sense of humour, he became tense, oppressed by his responsibilities, his eyes fixed on the danger ahead . . ."

"You must admit," interrupted L., "that the circumstances were unfavourable."

"Not so much at first. Remember the success of the van Zeeland Cabinet which was, after all, his Cabinet. Having ascended the throne in the midst of a world depression with its wave of unemployment, he realized that a government of national union, including the Socialists, might succeeed where a purely bourgeois government had failed. He chose young men, like himself, with a non-party man at their head. M. van Zeeland was given special powers to stabilize the franc and he did it successfully, thanks to a slight de-valuation, without bringing about a corresponding in-crease in the cost of living. Within a few months trade recovered and unemployment dropped by half. Van

Zeeland rallied a large majority. Everybody seemed delighted, barring a small minority of Communists and some ultra-Conservatives who could not be reconciled to the inclusion of Socialist Ministers in the Cabinet. That was in 1935, before the tragedy of Küssnacht. Why did it not last?"

"Political passions?" queried L. "The elections of May, '36, bringing with them an increase of Flemish extremism, Communism, not to mention Rexism?"

"Partly, but we must seek further than that. In a speech delivered in Brussels, the same year, on the occasion of the Centenary of the Provincial Law, the King had spoken of the reaction exerted upon Belgium by the social unrest prevailing in neighbouring countries. I remember some of his words: 'As these extreme currents come closer to our homes, they become calmer. We owe this to the soundness and suppleness of our institutions and to the sense of reality which is characteristic of our people'."

"That is just the kind of thing King Albert might have said," remarked L.

"He practically said it, but he used the word 'elasticity' instead of 'suppleness'. The manner might have been different, but the matter was the same. The key to every word and action of the son can be found in his father's words and actions. When Leopold repeated that his dearest wish was 'to seek inspiration' from Albert's ideas, 'in all questions and on all occasions,' it was no mere figure of speech."

"Let's go back," broke in L. "The trouble, you said, came from outside. We agree that internal difficulties were much aggravated by external difficulties. This

46

year '36, for instance: in March, Hitler denounces
Locarno and reoccupies the Rhineland, in May, 21
Rexists enter the Belgian Chamber, in October, the
King makes that famous speech, in which he declares
that Belgian external policy should henceforth be
entirely independent. Would his father have spoken in
the same way?"

"Remembering King Albert's policy from 1909 to
1914, I do not imagine that he could have talked
differently. That speech was not made in order to
pacify the Rexists. It was made in order to rally to the
common cause the adversaries of military reform,
including a number of Socialists and Catholics. I need
not remind you that the Belgian forces were in-
adequate, particularly since the reoccupation of the
Rhineland. Parliament would not agree to lengthen
the time of military service or to increase credits, as
long as the destinies of Belgium remained bound,
through her obligations under Locarno, with the destinies of France, and through France, with those of
Russia and Czecho-Slovakia. The King, in order to
remain faithful to his oath, had to find some means of
strengthening the country's defences, as his father had
endeavoured to do in 1912–1913. He had to choose
between a weak and divided Belgium dependent, not
only on the Allies' help, but also on the Allies' policy
which she could not hope to influence, and a stronger
and united Belgium, enjoying her neighbours' guarantee, but free to determine her own policy. With most
European statesmen, he still hoped that the catastrophe might be averted. Knowing that in any circumstances Belgium, on account of her position, would run

the gravest risks, he wished to do his utmost to avoid it, but his dominant preoccupation was to build up an army which could, at the worst, place a serious obstacle in the invader's path, and, at the best, prevent an invasion. There was never any doubt about the direction from which the blow might come. It was a choice between two evils. He chose the lesser and, for the life of me, I do not see what else he could have done."

"Besides," remarked L., "it was not his personal choice, it was the choice of the whole Government and of the great majority of the people. That October speech was not meant for publication. It was made before the Cabinet and published at the suggestion of its members because the Belgian Ministers hoped that it would re-establish a united front.[1]

"So far, so good. But what happened afterwards? Go on."

"Belgium had a perfect right to recover her freedom of action since Locarno had been denounced by one of the parties and since the arrangements concluded in March between Britain, France, Italy and herself were only temporary, pending the conclusion of a new Pact which did not materialize. She did not exercise this right. She merely explained her difficulties to her two former Allies—remember that Italy had by now joined the Axis—who recognized them and agreed explicitly and formally in the Franco-British Declaration of April 1937, that she was justified in taking the course she wished to take.[2] It was only after this agreement had been reached with them that a similar

[1] See further, p. 96. Appendix II.   [2] Appendix III.

agreement was negotiated with the Reich. It was hoped that, in the new disinterested position she occupied, Belgium might render some service in furthering the policy of appeasement which was pursued at the time by all the Powers, except of course Germany. It was generally recognized that the economic consequences of the last war and the peace settlement which followed were at the root of the trouble. This belief was strengthened by the fact that, after the conclusion of Locarno, the situation had considerably improved in Germany, and that the Nazis had only recovered from the severe setback they experienced at the time, owing to the considerable increase of unemployment caused by the world crisis of 1929–1930. This new line of thought which, if followed earlier, might have saved the world from another conflict by strengthening the moderate elements in Germany, is connected with the name of van Zeeland who was entrusted by Britain, France and America, with the task of pursuing an enquiry. The King was closely associated with the efforts of his Prime Minister."

"You are alluding to his letter of July 1937?"[1]

"You will notice that in this letter, the King goes even further than the van Zeeland report. He considered that the situation had deteriorated to such an extent that neither the lowering of tariffs nor any other 'partial measure' would suffice to cure the evil. I am quoting from memory: 'If we wish to avoid war we must have the courage to consider the question in its entirety and to face the great problems which threaten

[1] See Appendix IV.

E

THE PRISONER AT LAEKEN

mankind—distribution of raw material, currency, labour, and so on'."

"It was too late."

"There might still have been a chance in January, 1938, when the report was published and was heartily welcomed in many Allied quarters, more particularly among the leaders of the British Labour Party."

"Of pacifying Hitler?"

"Of removing some of the economic grievances which he had so successfully exploited. This hope was shared by many. If there was only a remote chance of success, the King wished to take it. His efforts never relaxed, even after van Zeeland's resignation, in November '37. The struggle went on with M. Janson at the head of affairs, later with M. Spaak. The diplomatic steps taken two years before bore fruit during the crisis of September 1938. Never was the nation so united and determined to resist. Delegations from all Parties called at the Palace, mobilization proceeded smoothly. No one thought of criticizing the policy of independence at that moment. On the contrary, it seemed justified by events. Did not an alliance, such as the one which bound Czecho-Slovakia to France, prove more dangerous than isolation? The King never left his study during this anxious time. He worked relentlessly, day and night.—Remember the tribute paid to him in the Chamber by Spaak[1]?—As soon as the crisis was over, he resumed his task. Either Munich would provide some delay, during which his plan might bring favourable results, or politics would once more defeat

[1] See Appendix VI.

economics and the catastrophe could no longer be avoided. To further the first, he pursued his studies with a small group of collaborators, laying down the foundations of an International Institute which might be consulted by the Powers if the spirit of co-operation prevailed. Against the second, he hastened military preparations in collaboration with his Minister of Defence and his military advisers. What more could he have done?"

"Neutrality in September 1939," added L., "was the policy of the whole nation. Once adopted, it could not be altered without a breach of international law and a breach of faith to the people, which might have caused serious internal reactions. No democratic government could have made such a change. The farthest M. Pierlot and M. Spaak could go—and it needed some courage—was to declare, in December '39, that the invasion of Holland would bring Belgium in. But why was there no Cabinet Meeting on May 10th, no meeting of Parliament, as in 1914?"

"Because there was no ultimatum to discuss. There was no time. According to the Constitution, the Sovereign was, in wartime, the Commander-in-Chief of the Army. His plain duty was to leave Brussels as soon as aggression had been ascertained and his Government had appealed to the guarantor Powers."

"Now we come to the story of the campaign, the Albert Canal, the K-W line, Sedan, the Scheldt, the Lys, the surrender . . . and we are in the dark . . ."

"The main question is: Was the surrender justified by events or not?"

At that moment, the door opened and a senior officer in a Belgian uniform stepped in, an old friend of L. The officer did not wait to be questioned. He declared that he came straight from Dunkirk. He had been at Belgian Headquarters on the afternoon when the "fatal decision" had been taken. He had been told nothing. He had only heard the news indirectly, just in time to make good his escape. The Belgian troops were still "full of fight", resistance might have been prolonged. Many units, he hoped, would disobey the order.

L. turned pale. I wished to put some questions to the visitor, but felt that I should no longer intrude on the conversation. On the pretext of a pressing engagement, I left at once.

The next day, on opening the paper, I experienced the worst shock of my life. Under the heading "A King and his Army", I read the following lines "from a Belgian correspondent": "A Belgian senior officer who saw King Leopold on Sunday night, only a few hours before the fatal decision was taken, and who succeeded in reaching England after the capitulation of the Belgian Army, made the following statement to me yesterday:—Nothing in the attitude of the King or in that of the Belgian troops gave any hint that capitulation was to be expected. As liaison officer with the French northern armies, I saw the King almost every day at General Headquarters. He was obviously much distressed by the sufferings of his people, but he was thinking like a soldier. The last time I saw him—about 8 p.m. on Sunday—he asked me what I thought of the situation, and in the remarks that he made there was nothing to give me the impression that he was going to force the Belgian Army to surrender.

"At that moment, in spite of the gravity of the situation, the idea that the Belgian Army would have to give up the struggle would not have occurred to anyone. Like the other Belgian officers, I could hardly believe the news when it spread like a trail of gunpowder the next morning. Officers, soldiers, civilians —everybody was thunderstruck; for everyone preferred the fighting and the bombing to submission in the face of the invader. What happened afterwards I cannot say, as I immediately left the Belgian zone to avoid falling into the enemy's hands."[1]

"Sunday night, a few hours before the fatal decision?" Sunday was May 26th. The decision was taken on the 27th at 4 p.m.

Would a "liaison officer with the French northern armies", whose headquarters were with the French, see the King "almost every day"? Who were "the other Belgian officers"? Surely, neither those who were in command of Belgian units at the front, nor those who were in close contact with the Staff, since the "fatal decision" had been taken by the Commander-in-Chief "a few hours later" after consulting the members of his Staff and in full agreement with them.

Did the views expressed by the writer faithfully reflect those of the "officers, soldiers and civilians" "thunderstruck" when they heard of the capitulation, or were they strongly influenced by the fact that he had spent most of his time, not with the Belgians, but

[1] *The Times*, May 30th, 1940.

with the French who apparently entertained strange illusions on the situation prevalent on the Belgian front?

These questions occurred to me later, when I knew the facts. For the present, the harm was done. With all the authority attached to his rank, and no doubt with the best intentions, this officer confirmed the legend that the surrender was not justified and had been kept secret for ulterior motives. It took weeks to dispel it and it may take months to show that King Leopold's actions, in May 1940, including the surrender of the army, have been consistent with his past actions, and that he remained faithful to that sense of duty and honour which dominated all his life from early childhood to the present day.

Chapter III
THE LEGEND

1. *Attitude of the Belgian Government*

THE LEGEND of King Leopold's premeditated treason started by M. Reynaud's speech spread far and wide. One thing only could have stopped it at that time, a peremptory contradiction from the leaders of the Belgian and British Governments. Unfortunately, neither of them were in a position to question the French Premier's veracity or to prevent the violent attacks provoked by his declarations.

During their last interview with their Sovereign, on May 25th, the Belgian Ministers had urged upon him the advisability, indeed the necessity, of leaving the front, in order to escape capture by the enemy and to pursue the fight with his Government, either from France or from England. This, according to them, was his duty as Head of the Executive. The King, on the other hand, had refused to leave his soldiers, convinced that his departure would break their morale and that his duty, as Commander-in-Chief, was to remain with his men to the last. In his order of the day of the same date, he had told them to pursue the fight and promised them that, whatever the issue of the desperate battle which was raging at the time, he would "share their fate." These two views, although both justifiable, could not be reconciled.

When the news of the surrender reached them in Paris, M. Pierlot and his colleagues had had no contact with Belgian Headquarters for two days. It is true that, when they had left, the fate of the Belgian Army already hung in the balance, but they did not know that it had been definitely sealed since the 26th. The only information they could obtain came from French sources and tallied with M. Reynaud's interpretation of the situation. They had tried to explain their difficulties to the French Premier, but had not found him disposed to listen to argument. They felt that it was not only their right but their duty to pursue the fight and, since all the available reserves of the Belgian Army were on French soil, they could only do so in conjunction with the French and with the co-operation of the French Government. They were assured that "negotiations" had actually taken place between their Sovereign and the enemy. They had no time to verify the fact. They had to make their position clear at once. It was to be now or never.

It was in these circumstances that, on the evening of the surrender, on May 28th, M. Pierlot broadcast a message to the Belgian people in which he said that disregarding the Government's unanimous advice, the King had opened "separate negotiations" with the enemy. He explained that these negotiations were unconstitutional, since they had not been sanctioned by the Government. He rightly declared that the Sovereign was no longer in a position to govern and that the Council of Ministers, in the name of the Belgian nation, wielded henceforth the only legal power. They would use it in order to "continue the struggle" at the side of the Allies, for the "liberation of the country." This speech, or rather the condemnation it implied, created the impression that the truth was still worse than M. Pierlot chose to reveal. This impression was confirmed by a garbled version published by a French agency, of the meeting of the 25th, at Wynendael, between the King and his four Ministers. It appeared from it that the question discussed was, not so much whether the Sovereign should leave his army, as that of the capitulation itself. The confidences made to the French Press by some Belgian deputies and senators did not improve matters: "We know that the people of Belgium believe that their King is guilty of treason"—his act "constitutes a unique stain upon our national history". Some Belgian journalists in Paris went so far as to "ask Frenchmen not to judge them after the fashion of their King. *Le Roi est mort. Vive la Belgique!*"

An account of these events has been given by M. van Cauwelaert, who was before the war President of the Belgian Chamber, and who accompanied the Ministers to Paris. "The Belgian Government," he writes, "taking its stand on incomplete information, which it had interpreted in good faith, but which it was impossible at that moment to check against the facts, was convinced that the King, going beyond the act of a simple unconditional military surrender, had allowed himself to be drawn into separate negotiations, and had treated with the enemy. . . . Unhappy circumstances compelled M. Pierlot to express himself publicly on this subject before French public opinion, without having been able to wait for further information".[1]

[1] *The Belgian Campaign*, p. 18 (Belgian-American Education Foundation). It should be added that M. Pierlot's speech saved the Belgian refugees in France from the severe punitive measures with which they were threatened at the time.

2. *Attitude of the British Government*

The position of the British Ministers was scarcely less difficult than that of their Belgian colleagues. The only Britisher who was in a position to criticize M. Reynaud's speech was Sir Roger Keyes, Special Liaison Officer with King Leopold. He had been with the King from the beginning of the campaign to the eve of the tragedy, and had kept his Government informed of the plight in which the Belgian Army found itself. He had left Belgium soon after the decision had been taken, and on his arrival in this country had urged his compatriots to "suspend judgment on a very gallant soldier until all the facts were known".

This was evidently the line which the British Government wished to take after hearing both M. Reynaud and Sir Roger. Mr. Churchill showed plainly in the House, on May 28th, that he did not wish, for the present, to endorse the French Premier's strictures and, later in the day, Mr. Duff Cooper followed the same line in a broadcast speech. He pointed out that the Belgian Army was no longer able to continue the fight: "They have fought very bravely, they have suffered very heavily, they have yielded only before overwhelming odds. This is no time for criticism or recrimination." He warned his listeners that, if they did anything to put the blame for present or future defeats upon their Allies, they would play into the hands of German propaganda, which had always done its utmost to divide Germany's opponents.

The Times, on the next day, published a moderate

article which criticized the neutral policy adopted by the Belgian Government, previous to the invasion, and attributed King Leopold's decision to "fear of Nazi brutality", but again emphasized the need for fuller information. "There is no reason to reject the plea for final judgment until the full facts are known."

Had this attitude been maintained, Belgium and her King might have been spared the full impact of public reprobation. But circumstances were unfavourable. It had been stated and it was firmly believed that the Belgian surrender had been the direct cause, instead of one episode, of the retreat upon Dunkirk, which had in fact already begun a few days before. It was also believed that only a small portion of the B.E.F., from 30,000 to 40,000 men, could be evacuated now that its "northern flank" was no longer protected. The rest would be killed or taken prisoner. Almost every Britisher had either a friend or a relation in Belgium or Northern France. King Leopold, through his "traitorous" and "cowardly" action, had thus made himself responsible for the death or imprisonment of this friend or relation. A wave of indignation swept over the country.

When the full diplomatic correspondence between the French and British Governments is published, we shall no doubt discover that M. Reynaud did not find Mr. Churchill's first declaration to his liking. He had done his best to obtain from M. Pierlot a declaration condemning the Sovereign's action, and wished the British to support him in this as in other matters. His power was shaken, how deeply, no one knew better than Mr. Churchill; he could not afford another moral defeat. The French Premier's scapegoat had served its purpose, and he wished it to go on serving its purpose. It was no use, he thought, preaching against recriminations and asking for the "full facts". Recriminations saturated France, at the time, and if they were not directed against King Leopold they would no doubt be directed against some one else. M. Reynaud was on the edge of the precipice. He had shown some courage and decision where others had failed to do so. Everything should be done to help him for the sake of France, of Britain, and of their common cause.

So it was that, a week later, on June 5th, Mr. Churchill in the same speech in which he announced to the House the successful withdrawal of 335,000 men from Dunkirk, referred once more to King Leopold. "Suddenly, without prior consultation, with the least possible notice, without the advice of his Ministers, and upon his own personal act, he sent a plenipotentiary to the German Command, surrendered his army and exposed our whole flank and means of retreat. (Cries of 'Shame!') I asked the House a week ago to suspend its judgment, but I do not feel any reason now exists why we should not form our own opinions upon this pitiful episode. (An Hon. Member: 'Treachery!')"

Had the reports made by Sir Roger Keyes been criticized by some military authority? Had the Premier gathered a different impression of the situation on the Belgian front, during the days preceding the surrender, from some other source? We may be sure in any case that he spoke as he spoke for some good purpose. The British Premier at least needed no scapegoat. The B.E.F. had fought valiantly and held its ground during the retreat necessitated by the break-through at Sedan. That was the main cause of the defeat and neither the British, nor the Belgians, were to blame for it.

To those who could read between the lines, Mr. Churchill's words appeared very different from those of M. Reynaud. He never referred to General Blanchard, and substituted "least possible notice" to "no warning", and "without advice" to "against the feeling." He never suggested premeditation or treason, not even "negotiations". To an impartial listener, he seemed to hint at a loss of nerve, a "fatal neutrality" leading to a fatal surrender.

But people were not disposed just then to read between the lines and to appreciate the way in which M. Reynaud's face was being saved for the common interest of the Allies. They cried "Shame!" and "Treachery!" like the impulsive M.P.s who heard the Premier's speech. Their country was in dire peril. In spite of its miraculous evacuation, their army had suffered important losses, if not in men, at least in material. After believing for months that the war would only require of them hard work and some priva-tions, they were threatened with immediate invasion and devastating bombardments. The *Blitz* had been revealed to them in all its gruesome horror. They did not wince, they held their ground, but they found a certain relief in venting their anger on the "great culprit", "the damned king".

I write these lines without bitterness. Far from

61

fostering a spirit of recrimination, I wish to put an end to it. But I believe that the best way to do so is to show when and how these recriminations began. Truth alone can dispel misunderstandings created by passion.

British Ministers had done their best to induce the public to turn its attention from the past to the future. They had urged it to leave King Leopold's reputation to the condemnation or vindication of history, not to speak, not to judge before all the facts were known. It was asking too much of human nature. The facts were not known, or known only to a few men who would not or could not give evidence. The accused himself had not been granted a hearing. Even the soundest people cannot suspend judgment or form an impartial opinion when dark clouds roll over the horizon torn by lightning. Danger and a fierce resolution to resist possessed every soul and shook every heart. It is not history, but legend which flourishes in such weather. The wonder is not that it spread so far and lasted so long, but that it kept within certain bonds and abated as soon as reliable evidence was produced. No greater tribute could be paid to the fairness of British public opinion.

3. *What a downfall!*

Before dealing with the legend which grew so rapidly around the name of King Leopold, I must apologize for introducing a personal note.

Since my arrival in this country in 1908, I had devoted most of my time to the improvement of Anglo-Belgian relations. I had written and spoken in Belgium on English subjects and in Great Britain on

Belgian subjects. I had been closely associated in the work undertaken in London, during the last war, to keep the English-speaking public informed of the achievements of the Belgian Army and the ordeal to which my compatriots were subjected under enemy occupation. Ever since, I had endeavoured to spread the knowledge of Belgian history, art and literature in a series of books, lectures and articles. I had made more friends in this country than in my own and built up for myself the reputation of an *"anglophile enragé."*

It would have been only natural that, since I had been associated with the events of 1914, I should also have been associated with those of 1940. As I had, somewhat undeservedly, shared the praise, I expected to share the blame. Lest anyone should suspect that the statements I make in this chapter are inspired by some personal grievance, I should like to say that, in the course of last summer, I never read or heard a word directed against me, although I had before and since the outbreak of war published a book and written articles in which I defended the Belgian neutral attitude. On the contrary, several correspondents, some of whom unknown to me, took the trouble to send me messages of sympathy and had the extreme generosity of refraining from expressing at the same time any criticism directed against my King or Government. The only remark which rankles in my mind was made by a friend who, after recalling the glorious days of 1914, murmured almost under his breath: "What a downfall!" The words were not meant to hurt, but they did, because they were true and because I could not show, at the time, that the downfall was undeserved.

Some months before the tragedy, I had been invited by a learned Society to deliver an address in London on "Belgium and the War", in which I intended to explain how my country had been compelled by circumstances to adopt a neutral attitude. After May 10th, I altered my notes in order to show that the Belgians were as good as their word and proved by their military resistance that, contrary to common belief, they had never given way to fear. On the 28th, in the early morning, the telephone bell rang. I lifted the receiver without suspecting that the words I was going to hear would be of any significance. The Society's Secretary asked me what I intended to do about my address, which I was to give two days later. As I expressed some astonishment, she said:

"Haven't you heard?"

"What has happened?"

"King Leopold has surrendered with his whole Army."

The sinking feeling which I experience when a bomb falls close to my house is not comparable to the reaction which these words provoked in me. After a moment, I was able to shout.

"I don't believe it!"

"Well, it's in the news."

"That's no sufficient reason. There are many rumours . . ."

"I mean official news. . . . Reynaud talking on the wireless . . ."

There was a longer pause, after which I apologised

for my rudeness and asked the Secretary to wait until the evening. I must think it over.

A few hours later, I heard M. Pierlot speak. Belgium was still at war. I decided to keep my engagement.

I had nothing to go by except the French and Belgian Premiers' speeches. I did not know that, up to the 27th, the King had faithfully followed the instructions of the French Command. I did not know that the surrender was inevitable and justified by military necessities. I did not know that it was a purely military act involving no diplomatic negotiations. I did not know that the Allies had been warned repeatedly since May 20th, and that, if the last warning had not reached French and British Headquarters, neither the Belgian Commander-in-Chief nor his staff were to blame for it. I did not even know that the decision of the Belgian Staff had been unanimous and that the Belgian units which received the order obeyed at once. Indeed, some rumours had already reached me that this was not the case. Treason was in the air when I faced my audience. To this overwhelming belief I could only oppose my blind confidence in a man whose every action I had followed since his early youth, but with whom I had only had one hour's intimate talk.

This is the summary of what I said, at the time: "I do not attach much importance to the rumour according to which King Leopold had pro-German tendencies because he did not always agree with the decisions of the French Generals or even because of the difficulty of getting him to combine his strategy with the strategy of the Allies. These things always happen when a Sovereign is in charge of a national army. They happened very definitely, during the battle of the Yser, between King Albert and General Foch. We have not one scrap of evidence of a pro-German leaning going on for years, or of a dark plot hatched for weeks. The only evidence in our hands, and I think it will be confirmed by history, is that after a series of retreats, brought about by the terrible break through the French forces at Sedan, the King, threatened with encirclement, lost all hope. He had witnessed terrible scenes, he had lost half his army, he had seen the refugees thronging the roads and mowed down by machine-guns. It was too much for him. If it was too much for him, why did he not follow his Ministers when they begged him to leave the army, and why did he not come over here? That is the mystery. We are still in the dark and we lack information.''

This statement was inaccurate in two respects. I assumed that there might have been some truth in the current allegation that the King had disagreed with the instructions given him by the Generalissimo, and I exaggerated the influence which his personal feelings, at the sight of the scenes he witnessed, exerted on his final decision.

If I do not resist the temptation of quoting these lines, it is not because I wish to show that, on the main question, I had been a good prophet, but because I wish to render homage to the fairmindedness which prevailed among my audience. Not only did its members give me a patient and almost friendly hearing, but in the discussion which followed nothing was said by them which could make my own position more painful. One of them, the distinguished editor of a well-known weekly, went so far as to say that he felt greatly in my debt. This, at a time when the fate of the B.E.F. still hung in the balance on the beach of Dunkirk!

This personal experience did not, however, blind me to the fact that the event of May 27th had, for the time being, ruined all the efforts which I had made to bring more closely together the country of my birth and the country of my adoption. Where was the Anglo-Belgian Union to which I had devoted most of my life? I had only to read the papers and to listen to the woeful tales of the Belgian refugees to realise it. What a downfall since the glorious days of Liège, Antwerp and the Yser, since King Albert's flying visit to London in 1917, and his state reception after the last war! He had, according to his own words, been "cornered into heroism". His son, whom he had so carefully prepared to succeed him, had been cornered into surrender. Those who remembered the heroic resistance of the Belgian Army and the suffering and endurance of the Belgian people, during those years, were particularly bitter. Many who had found excuses for the failure of Norway and Holland, even for the non-resistance of Denmark, could not forgive the Belgian surrender. These nations had been neutral during the last war, they were unprepared and riddled with Nazi intrigues. But Belgium had betrayed all expectations. The old ally had first turned neutral, and later deserted his post in the crucial hour of dire need. Belgium who had held the gate at Liège, had opened it on Dunkirk. Her king, her soldiers, who had once been shown as examples to the world, were now held in contempt. Every memory added to the general sense of grievance. Past virtues, instead of alleviating it, aggravated the present guilt. The word "Treachery!" shouted across the House during the Premier's speech found echoes in every English home. All previous disappointments dwindled into insignificance before this dramatic collapse. The trusted friend had joined hands with the old enemy.

Leopold III was well known in this country. He had spent two years at Eton, and had been strongly influenced by English life. He spoke the language fluently. When still Duke of Brabant, in 1933, he had roused great interest in colonial circles by an address delivered in London before the African Society, in which he had urged that Great Britain and Belgium should collaborate in the preservation of tropical nature. His interest in economic questions and their relation to international affairs had also been noticed, and his appeal to British co-operation, on the occasion of his State visit of November, 1937, had to a great extent dispelled the misunderstandings provoked, in certain quarters, by the change which had taken place in Belgian policy, a few months before.[1]

For all these reasons, for the personal friendship which bound him to King George, for his handsome appearance, for the deep sympathy people had felt for him when they had heard of King Albert's death and of the tragic accident of Küssnacht, he was considered "the most popular foreign Sovereign" in this country. He shared, among young girls, the hero-worship lavished on celebrated cinema stars. His picture was

[1] See Appendix V.

familiar to all. The most trifling incident in his life was faithfully recorded and embellished in the gossip columns of the popular press.

All this well-founded or superficial popularity now turned against him. Within a day, the hero became a traitor, and the brave, handsome young man a decadent and effeminate coward. The vilification was as violent, among certain people, as the idealization had been foolish. The celebrated Partridge cartoon showing the Kaiser and King Albert against a background of ruined and burning villages—"You have lost everything."—"Not my soul!"—was taken down from the wall and replaced by a drawing showing Leopold, covered with German decorations and bowing before Hitler who was presenting him with a castle. Instead of the "King Albert's Book," to which almost every well-known British and French writer, musician and artist, had sent enthusiastic contributions, appeared a collection of violent caricatures and accusations. Maeterlinck used some rash words which are better forgotten. Some eminent men in this country, including Mr. Lloyd George and Mr. H. G. Wells, were waylaid by the same impulse. To smaller men, "Leopold" was fair game. He could not defend himself, he was supposed to have been "deposed" or "disowned" by his own people and Government, and those who could have defended him were compelled to remain silent, on account of the position they occupied, or because they could not produce the necessary evidence. La Fontaine's fable was re-enacted: "*Tout le monde cria haro! sur le baudet.*"

69

4. *Treachery!*

The Leopoldian legend may be divided into three parts, the first dealing with the "hero's" character, entourage and sympathies, the second with his "neutralism" and the policy inaugurated in 1936, and the third with the manner in which this supposed character and policy influenced his conduct of military operations from May 10th to May 28th 1940. The two last parts will be the subject of later chapters. Let us confine ourselves here to the analysis of the first.

In this analysis, I shall not mention the wildest rumours which reached me by word of mouth for fear of being accused of exaggeration. I shall only record a few of those which found their way into the British Press. I am well aware that if I were able to include some which appeared in France and America at the time, I should be able to present to the reader a far more picturesque and vivid collection, for the Leopoldian legend started in France, under the impulse given by M. Reynaud, and most of its episodes recorded here came from across the Channel.

Not wishing to provoke any controversy, I shall quote neither the names of the authors, when the articles are signed, nor the names of the papers in which they appeared. If anyone wishes me to produce this information, I shall be ready to do so as long as the bulging file which lies in front of me escapes destruction.

On May 31st, the Havas agency issued the following communiqué which was reproduced in most English papers. To give it more weight, the French agency

70

quoted "sources in close touch with the refugee Belgian Government": "The treachery of King Leopold was not only military but was an organized and premeditated felony. It is now revealed that, since the beginning of the war, Leopold had forbidden his Ministers to leave Belgian soil, particularly for France, so as to avoid any personal contacts there. He refused, on any account, to present himself before Parliament before taking up the leadership of the army, as his father had done in 1914. He also refused to condemn the invaders in a radio speech. From the start of hostilities, Leopold showed signs of a defeatist spirit which would have led an ordinary citizen into severe trouble . . ."

The fact that the official French agency took the responsibility of this statement two days after the British Government, through the Prime Minister and the Minister of Information, had advised the public to "postpone judgment" is one of the reasons which leads me to believe that their declarations had not been well received in Paris.

As for the statement itself, no one with any knowledge of Belgian affairs could for one moment consider it seriously. Ministers are not subject to military discipline in constitutional countries even in wartime. As a matter of fact, one member of the Government, M. Gutt, had been in England before the interview of May 25th. Considering that Belgium had been attacked without ultimatum or declaration of war, on May 10th, the Sovereign could not possibly spare the time to "present himself before Parliament" before joining his Headquarters. King Albert would have

71

acted exactly in the same way in the same circumstances. His son had issued, on the 10th, a categorical proclamation to his people: "Between sacrifice and dishonour the Belgians will not hesitate in 1940 as they did not hesitate in 1914. . . . I intend to remain faithful to my constitutional oath. As my father did in 1914, I have placed myself at the head of our Army, with the same faith, the same conscience." But he did not "broadcast" it—there lay the evident proof of his premeditated crime!

"From the start of hostilities . . ."? How could anyone "in touch with the Belgian Government" ascertain this? Besides, if there had been premeditation why should the Commander-in-Chief have waited so long? Had he sold the pass on the 10th or on the 15th, the Allies would have found themselves in a far more critical situation.

This piece of blatant propaganda was more worthy of Berlin than of Paris. It was a bad start, but it worked. Anything might have worked.

On the same day (May 31st) an important British weekly published the following appreciation under the title: "Leopold the Renegade": "It is just over a fortnight ago that Leopold of Belgium begged the Allies to go to his assistance, a request which was promptly and generously met. Leopold's way of showing his gratitude was to go over to the Germans and leave his helpers—and his own brave people—in the lurch. This foul desertion came as a heavy and unexpected blow. Perhaps we are culpable for not having expected it, as Leopold has a good measure of Hohenzollern blood in his veins. The best—because it is the

wittiest and most blistering comment on the crowned
Judas Iscariot, emanated from a distinguished journalist: 'For the next two hundred years no parent will
christen his son Leopold.' That can be his epitaph;
for he is dead to his countrymen for ever, dead to the
friends whom he betrayed, and dead, presumably, to
what passes for a conscience in a man at once so vain
and cowardly."

Diplomatic correspondents vied with one another to
explain the mystery. Some dwelt on the influence of
the King's sister, the Princess of Piedmont, who was
herself prompted by her husband or, worse still, by
the Duce; others on that of Queen Elisabeth, the
King's mother, who was by birth a Bavarian Princess.
Few remembered that she had been at the side of
King Albert, behind the front, all through the last
war, and had devoted herself heart and soul to the care
of the wounded, breaking off all relations with her
German family which was separated from her by "a
curtain of iron". During the crisis of 1938 and the
first months of the war, she had once more visited the
army and ingratiated herself with the soldiers. What
sinister motive prompted her to do so? For a short
time, the faint shadow of a German girl, the unavoidable vamp, floated over the scene. She vanished
as suddenly as she had come, for no apparent reason.

On June 8th, a long article was published in another
weekly signed "A Belgian Correspondent". It began
by denouncing the policy of non-commitment recognized by the Franco-British Declaration of 1937, as
being the main cause of the "Belgian tragedy".
It went on complaining of the "high-handed fashion"

in which the Sovereign had, in recent years, lectured his Ministers, and representing M. Pierlot and M. Spaak as pliant tools in his hands. It alluded to some mysterious rumours of a "royal military dictatorship" backed by the Rexist party, and concluded with the following remarks: "And now the very consequences of that policy has enabled the King to order that capitulation to the enemy which, of all conceivable possibilities, seemed to the entire Belgian people the most unthinkable, the most disastrous, and the most degrading. King Leopold was in a position to commit this act because, at the very beginning of the war, he insisted on being made, himself, Commander-in-Chief of the army. Again, his ministers shouldered a heavier responsibility than they knew in pandering to the royal desires."

In order, no doubt, to convince his readers of his "dispassionate attitude", the author had denied in one of his opening sentences the accusation of "calculated treachery". He ended, however, on a different note. The suggestion was made, not for the first time, that the reign of Leopold III should end with the capitulation of the Belgian Army, that he should not be declared "incapable of reigning" as long as he was in the power of the enemy, but formally "deposed", and that the Allies should see to it that the Belgian monarchy were replaced, after the war, by another form of government which could "give a firm and intelligent lead" to the country.

Who should give this lead? In order to discover the name of the future President of the Belgian Republic, I wrote to the paper, pointing out some blatant inaccuracies and challenging the anonymous "Belgian Correspondent" to name himself. My letter was published with unfailing courtesy, but the challenge was not taken up.

Thus the legend developed. M. van Zeeland, who had initiated the policy of non-commitment, was represented as the last champion of collective security. Complacent ministers, a restless public opinion, a gagged Press dominated from the Royal Palace; at Laeken, a German mother; in Rome, a Fascist sister; in Brussels a defeated and depleted Rexist party wielding formidable power. The King, who had on several occasions, publicly dissociated himself from M. Degrelle's politics, represented as his best friend and accomplice, another "tool in the hands of Hitler and Mussolini."

"We shall soon hear," declared another paper, a few days later (June 16th), "of the thirty pieces of silver with which King Leopold is to be rewarded. Hitler is at present drawing a plan for uniting Holland, Belgium and Luxembourg into a new puppet state. And Leopold, acting as the puppet of Hitler, will be offered the united crown."

Verse itself contributed to the legend. Two well-known poets burst into croaking song.

On June 22nd, another writer delivered the following verdict: "Young King Leopold, unlike his father, was anti-French, and what was more complicating—anti-Democratic; and his early Fascist feelings were focused by certain untoward feminine associations which, in retrospect, seem to have been nourished by Mussolini as well as by the Nazis. He was befooled and befogged—even bewitched. It is better to be wicked than weak."

King Leopold's accusers were divided into two schools, the one treated him as a coward, the other as a traitor. On June 2nd, in a Sunday paper, Mr. Lloyd George surpassed himself in combining the two accusations into one remarkable piece of oratorical invective: "You can rummage in vain through the black annals of the most reprobate Kings of the earth to find a blacker and more squalid sample of perfidy and poltroonery than that perpetrated by the King of the Belgians. . . . If Belgium ever again tolerates such a monarch, she will share his disgrace." M. Reynaud's eloquence pales before this article.

The same issue of the paper contains an account of a séance held a few hours after the capitulation of the Belgian Army in the course of which Queen Astrid "appeared" to "four London spiritualists." It was first thought that the apparition, or "transfiguration", was due to the Queen's "distressed condition" caused by "the sufferings of the Belgian people. The news of the King's defection points to a more personal reason." —No doubt, the ghost of the Queen denounced the traitor and confirmed the abuse heaped upon him in the leading article.

It has become possible to preserve a detached attitude before those strange manifestations of collective imagination. It was not so easy to do so at the time.

M. Reynaud had set the ball rolling and bears the chief responsibility. Those who followed his lead, as long as the facts had not been published, cannot be blamed for expressing freely their indignation. But only a frank and sincere apology can clear those who went on kicking the ball after the whistle of the umpire had been heard and a foul declared.

There were more moderate appreciations given by men who had really the right to speak, having been in personal contact with King Leopold, and having had some opportunity of appreciating his faults and virtues. Unfortunately, in the light of recent events, the former were given such a prominent place that the picture became curiously distorted. The King was a "sad man" with "no sense of fun, let alone a sense of humour." He had never laughed "since the tragic death of his consort—that gay and lovable women, Queen Astrid." Leopold III was "morbid and intro-spective, of a violent and uncontrollable temper." Had he been gay, instead of sad, he would no doubt have been described as heartless; had he never shown his temper, he would have been called effeminate. The appreciation ended with words of condescending pity for the monarch whose "brief reign has been indeed a tragedy both for himself and for the world," but the reader could not help thinking that the words "mor-bid," "introspective," "violent," "obsessed," had some hidden and sinister meaning.

The simple minded evoked the infamy of Judas, the refined and literary dallied with the tragic image of the melancholy, ill-balanced Prince of Denmark.

5. *The Legend Illustrated*

The "King Albert's Book" had been illustrated by a number of British artists, Walter Crane, Dulac,

Lavery, Partridge, Poynter, Shannon, Rackham, among them. The Leopoldian legend did not lack illustrators. Art adorns heroism, caricature exposes treachery.

These pictures are worth mentioning because they describe even better than the written word, the systematic vilification to which the royal prisoner at Laeken was subject during this period.

No hero in armour, crossing the fire, this time, no St. George lying prone, close to the dead dragon, no defiant figure brandishing the flag, no bleeding Belgium breaking her bonds or stretching out her hands in a pathetic appeal to the world; but a large motor car bringing the Führer to the edge of the sea, while a small Leopold, between two corpulent chauffeurs, touches his cap in an apologetic manner: "Sorry, Sir, this is as far as I can guide you, Sir!" (May 30th); or John Bull, with a dagger stuck in his back ("from Leopold") turning in amazement towards a wounded boy in wooden shoes (Belgium) shouting: "Lead on!" (May 29th); or again, the ghost of Albert reproving the same Leopold waving a white flag over Belgian soil: "My son, it's unbelievable." (May 28th.)

Within a few days, Leopold III had become, not only the arch-traitor, but the acknowledged leader of the international fifth column, and for many months to come his name was to be associated with those of Quisling, Pétain and—after the attitude of the latter had provoked a certain reaction—the infamous Laval. Holland also had her fifth columnists, but, fortunately for her, they did not attract so much attention. The King's picture appeared side by side with

78

those of Quisling and of the notorious Rexist leader, Degrelle (July 7th). A few days before, thousands of Englishmen, opening their evening paper, could see him prostrate at the feet of the two triumphant Dictators, between Quisling and a black-coated figure inscribed "Bordeaux," while an infuriated Poilu (France) spat on his back. This was on June 25th, a week after Marshal Pétain had decided to ask Hitler for an armistice, and M. Reynaud had relinquished the reins of Government.

The climax of the legend was reached when an illustrated paper published a photograph of King Leopold "in 1935 before his wife's death", side by side with that of another personage, Gustav Oldendorff, who was supposed to have impersonated the Sovereign since the Küssnacht accident, in which the real King had been killed: "This plan", said the anonymous author of this remarkable story, "was worked by Hitler himself, and has been applied to other Kings, Generals and statesmen." The likeness was certainly remarkable and one can but admire the ingenuity of the explanation. It solved the question which had been puzzling many people, and which I took the liberty of raising in the previous chapter. How can a man behave as King Leopold behaved since his early youth, and act as he was supposed to have acted? Why did I not realize that my King was no longer my King when I talked with him, but a Nazi agent who had so cleverly deceived the entourage, including his mother, his children, his Ministers, his whole household and his whole people? Why did I not guess that "the appeals to the Pope, to Queen Wilhelmina (*sic*) and to the

Allies were all part of a scheme to give Hitler time," and that Leopold-Oldendorff did not give in "until the Allies were truly in the trap" into which he had drawn them by his "anguished" appeal? Truly, to use the words of this remarkable contribution to the Leopoldian legend, "this fifth column business goes beyond the human conception and even beyond the realms of fantasy!"

Let us, therefore, beware! Churchill might be spelt Kirchhügel and Roosevelt, Rosenfeldt. All they are doing might conceal a hidden purpose and their efforts might lead us, not to glorious victory, but to shameful defeat. The final act will be played when the Allied Armies enter Berlin, so that the gates of the German capital might close upon them. As the French say: *Un homme averti en vaut deux.*

6. *"This Fifth Column Business"*

The more one examines the conditions which favoured the growth and development of the Leopoldian legend, the more one wonders at the combination of adverse circumstances which converted a military defeat into an act of premeditated treason. There was not only the tension resulting from the critical military situation and the threat of invasion, the dreadful implications of the French Premier's indictment and the impossibility of contradicting it, there was also the fact that certain events which occurred during the invasion of Norway and Holland had given an extraordinary importance to Nazi intrigues and secret activities.

In the first instance, we had seen well-defended ports oppose no resistance to German aggression owing to Quisling and other pro-German agents; in the other, we had learnt that the heroic resistance of the Dutch army had been hampered and, in certain instances, completely checked by German residents and their paid agents. By the time hostilities started in Belgium, the fifth column was the subject of all conversations. That it was an essential part of Nazi technique in Allied as well as in neutral countries cannot be questioned, but some people with a liking for mystery stories were inclined to accept too readily exaggerated versions of actual events. The spy craze of the last war was nothing compared with the fifth column craze of this one.

Now, the Belgian campaign started with some unfortunate accidents. There was a bridge, on the Albert Canal, which should have been blown up, and an important fort commanding the Meuse which should not have been captured. The Belgians explained these accidents, but their explanations reached this country after the one given in certain French military quarters; and that explanation implied grave if not criminal negligence. Even after Sedan, some writers were still contending that most of the Allies' reverses were due to the non-destruction of a certain bridge "in front of Maastricht."

Then came a rumour that the advance of the British and French armies into Belgium had been hampered by the fact that the roads were crowded with refugees, and that the Belgian authorities had taken no action in the matter. This was contradicted later by British witnesses, but the bad impression prevailed, especially because this overcrowding which had not seriously disturbed military communications during the advance—which was foreseen in case of invasion—became a real difficulty during the retreat, ordered by the French Command on May 15th, which had not been foreseen.

After the return of the B.E.F., further reports of enemy activity behind the front in Belgium and Northern France were widely circulated. Similar reports of secret signalling and tampering with telephonic communications had already reached me during the last war. They always occur during a campaign because, in every country, the enemy manages to maintain a certain number of spies. Out of ten genuine cases, rumour makes a thousand. Besides, the military mind is suspicious of civilians, more particularly of foreign civilians. The number of these suspects and of their misdeeds increases in proportion to the disappointment caused by reverses. They afford a convenient excuse and allow men who have undergone the ordeal of defeat to vent their temper on those who contributed, or who were suspected of contributing to it. It is easier to say that the army's lines of communications were tampered with by fifth columnists than to admit that they could no longer be protected against the attacks of enemy parachutists or the raids of mechanized units.

As a matter of fact, there was considerably less fifth column activity in Belgium than in any other country invaded by the Nazis in Western Europe.[1] This

[1] *Cf.* Gordon Beckles: "In Belgium, however, no widespread damage by fifth columnists was yet evident. The Nazis had found more promising material for treason in Holland than in Belgium" (p. 27).

activity never interfered with military operations or influenced the action of the Government. In spite of the fantastic statistics produced by certain writers, the number of Germans in Belgium, on May 10th, was not abnormally high,[1] and they were all placed under supervision. For years past every foreigner arriving in Belgium, unless French, Dutch or Luxemburger, had to register at the local police station. He was placed under the control of the *Sûreté Publique*, a special branch of the Ministry of Justice, which alone could grant permits to reside in a determined locality for a limited period of time, and which had the right to request any undesirable to leave the country, or even to proceed to expulsion. The Government had, besides, organized a special Commission, similar to the Tribunals instituted in this country at the beginning of the war, before which any political refugee could appear, if he so desired, to produce proofs of his *bona fide*.

From September, 1939, all those who had infringed regulations by coming into the country without permit, or appeared otherwise suspicious characters, were either forbidden to leave their residence or interned in special camps.

After the experience of the last war, the State possessed all the necessary means to repress spying, and they were used drastically. From September '39 to May '40, about forty spies, acting for Germany, were arrested and imprisoned. On May 10th, no less than 1,650 suspects were rounded up and sent to France. There were only 500 Belgians among them. The magistrate responsible for this measure, M.

[1] About 200,000.

Ganshof, the *Auditeur-Général*, was the first victim of Nazi persecution, when he was compelled to leave France and return to Belgium after the French Armistice.

This did not prevent the legend of the Belgian fifth column from spreading concurrently with that of the King's treason. Indeed, the two were soon linked together, and it was suggested that the pro-Nazi leanings of the Sovereign were largely responsible for the activity of spies or defeatists. Many people still believe that Belgium was honeycombed with German or pro-German agents, and that her defeat was due to the reluctance of the terrorized authorities to taking the necessary measures at the right moment. Did not the King give the example? Let us therefore draw a lesson from the Belgian tragedy. Let us beware of the "Quislings, the Leopolds and such-like Lavals!"[1]

7. *The Black Baroness*

Legends must necessarily find a literary expression. When they are founded on reality, they produce noble tragedies or great poems such as the *Iliad*, the *Morte d'Arthur* or the *Chanson de Roland*. When they are built on more shaky foundations, they produce works

---

[1] In a recent book, prefaced by Dorothy Thompson, M. W. Fodor repeats this fantastic accusation: In November 1939, "King Leopold, tipped off by German emissaries and by a German lady friend, rushed to the Hague." . . . On May 6th 1940, "the Dutch were more nervous than the Belgians, because the Fifth Column worked better in Brussels . . ." On the eve of invasion, leaves in the Army were restored by the "Fifth-Column-inspired part of the Belgian military leadership"! (*The Revolution is On*, pp. 24–29.)

of inferior quality—melodramas and thrillers. Out of all the loud gossip, whispered rumour and scandal-mongering which soon clustered around M. Reynaud's indictment, emerged Mr. Dennis Wheatley's *The Black Baroness*. There may be other stories woven around the same theme already printed or in the course of printing, but Mr. Wheatley's is so typical that their authors must excuse me if I do not record them here. A literary criticism is not an encyclopædia. It is enough to choose a good specimen of the species you wish to describe. *The Black Baroness* is a specially good specimen and Mr. Wheatley may be hailed as the Homer, or the Ossian, of the Leopoldian legend. It is a title that few will envy him.

His book is a hybrid product where history and fiction are blended together. It shows what Mr. St. John Ervine has called a "celluloid mentality", an unquenchable thirst for information and an enormous appetite for excitement. On the first page, appears the sub-title, "a novel", on the second, the honoured names of distinguished officers "the earliest readers of my unpublished work". It is scarcely believable that such a work should not have been submitted to the censorship. It is still more difficult to understand how and why the censorship allowed its publication.

It belongs to fiction in some of its aspects. The hero, Gregory, and the heroine, Erika, are certainly fictitious. So are their exciting adventures, including their efforts at thwarting the intrigues of the Gestapo, and their secret interview with King Leopold at Belgian Headquarters. The Baroness herself begins as a character in a novel, to assume in the last chapters the

features of the notorious Madame de Portes. Her
activity ranges from Norway to Bordeaux, and every
head of every State she cares to visit falls the victim of
her somewhat overripe charms. But on the other hand,
military events are more or less accurately described
in their geographical setting, and the names of the
King, of his mother, Queen Elisabeth, and certain
members of the supposed entourage are printed without the slightest scruple. Such books used to be called
romans à clef, because their authors were careful to
disguise their characters, but here the key is placed
in the reader's hand so that he may be spared the
effort of guessing.

M. Reynaud's indictment was both untrue and unfair, but it had at least the merit of a certain frankness.
Its author took the risk and reaped the sad results of
his rash words. But Mr. Wheatley played for safety.
He may always plead that his work is a "novel" and
that, in this free country, the freedom of the artist
should not be restricted. M. Reynaud treated King
Leopold as an enemy and showed no pity. But Mr.
Wheatley—or Mr. Wheatley, through the good and
kind Erika, "Leopold's new girl-friend"—does not
even spare the King the humiliation of his sympathy:
"He's nearly at the end of his tether. He's one of those
artistic, highly-strung people, he adored his wife,
Astrid, you know, and he's never really got over her
loss. . . . He knows perfectly well that he ought to fight
on, and the memory of his father seems to haunt
him; but so many people round him have always told
him that Hitler is great and wise and good. He feels
that every Belgian is being as badly bombed as he is

and that he only has to ask the magnanimous Führer
for honourable terms and he'll get them and save his
people from this nightly horror. That's why he sent
his Cabinet to Paris. . . . He's not even mentioned
what he's feeling to his Generals or to the high Allied
officers who are attached to his person; he's terrified
of what they might say to him. . . . He's a pathetic
figure, showing a brave face each day and breaking
down each night. . . . When I left him he was going
to turn in, and his doctor had promised to give him a
really strong dose of medinal . . ."

Of course, the whole thing is absurd. It is utterly
absurd that a Commander-in-Chief should be attended
at his headquarters by a number of "camp-followers",
including two women, a British Secret Service agent,
and two German envoys who had come in the hope of
extorting his signature. It is still more absurd that the
monarch should confide all his troubles to a perfect
stranger, declare that he is "sick to death of being
told that his father was a lion-hearted saint," and
give a regular exhibition of nerves, "his hands round
his knees," "rocking from side to side," or "wearily
mopping his face": "What am I to do?" he asks
Gregory, "who *am* I to believe? I don't know."
And, after hearing a few bombs drop in the neigh-
bourhood: "I can't! I can't! . . . no, no—*no*!" It is
supremely ridiculous that, at the crucial moment,
when Erika throws herself on the King to prevent him
from signing the fatal paper, the Baroness should shoot
her down from behind a curtain, and appear on the
scene, revolver in hand: "Erika had lost consciousness
and the King now stood with her limp form in his

arms. 'You've killed her! You've killed her!' he screamed hysterically. . . . 'I'll have you shot for this . . . .' "

All this and much more is offensive in the extreme, in the saga of the Black Baroness. It is, besides, written in a style unworthy of the author.

Had it appeared in the form of a short story, soon after the event, it might have been passed as a piece of sensational journalism and excused as such. After all, a man must live, and business is business. But it is a longish work, written several months after the Belgian campaign—the preface is dated, September 1940—when some of the facts had already been published. To strike the iron while it is hot at the risk of burning one's fingers is one thing. To rekindle the fire with a bundle of slanderous gossip and call it a bonfire, in order to avoid trouble, is another. *The Black Baroness* is blacker than she is painted.

8. *King and Country*

Attempts were made in the Press and in public speeches to dissociate the Belgian people from the actions of their King. The Belgians were told that they could in no way be rendered responsible for their Sovereign's treachery, that their army had fought valiantly, that the civil population had merely been the victim of the policy of the evil man who had abused his constitutional power and violated his constitutional oath. This attitude was prompted, partly by the desire of the believers in the Leopoldian legend not to inflict unnecessary pain on the Belgians residing in Britain or who had sought refuge in this country, and partly by the prejudice existing among all Republicans, either Belgian or British, against any initiative taken by the Crown. "It is plain," wrote H. G. Wells, as late as October 24th, "that King Leopold has to be tried by his own people and the world for what many of us think was his deliberate treason to them and us, and either acquitted as a foolish weakling, unfit to govern a brave people, or else condemned and executed. . . . If he is guilty he should die. What is one life to the sweetening of the world by such an execution!" I have too much respect for Mr. Wells's intelligence to suppose that he wrote these lines seriously. As a true *Jacobin*, he seized this pretext of upbraiding a crowned head, and did not care to inquire whether the indictment was well founded or not. What is one life, what is one head, as long as the crown it wears rolls down with it!

Crises such as the one through which the Belgians passed last summer reveal the best and the worst in human nature. The game of vilifying King Leopold apparently paid in France, before and after the armistice. It was consequently pursued in England, but somehow it fell flat. I suppose that this lack of success was mainly due to the fact that the majority of Britishers are at heart sincere royalists. It is one thing to denounce a foreign Sovereign; it is another to hear him denounced by his own subjects.

I understand the attitude of sincere republicans who for rational or political reasons wish to do away with kingship altogether. I understand still better the attitude of sincere royalists who for traditional or sentimental reasons wish to preserve it. But I fail to understand those who are, at the same time, attracted by the glamour of court life and ready to destroy it, equally eager to receive honours and to accept the dishonour of the Sovereign who conferred them, moved one day by vapid snobbishness and the next by scandalmongering. That the King has to render account of his actions to human and divine justice, like anyone else, is, I believe, accepted by all. He is, in a democratic country, the first citizen of the nation, the symbol of its unity, of its continuity, of its essential characteristics. But that he should be deprived of the protection afforded by the law to the least of these citizens is a paradox difficult to explain. The doctrine that the Crown should be sheltered from attacks is justified, not on account of royal privilege, but on account of popular privilege. He who slanders the Sovereign slanders the humblest of his subjects, lowers the prestige of the whole people and stains the honour of the whole nation.

This is particularly true in constitutional countries where the Crown no longer possesses its old prerogatives, and can only "warn and advise" the Government. If, under the Constitution, members of Parliament enjoy a certain degree of immunity, as representatives of part of the people, the King should enjoy at least the same immunity as the representative of the whole people. He may certainly be the subject of criticism, but care should be taken that this criticism should be supported by facts or, if the facts are unobtainable, should stop as soon as they are obtainable.

To question this principle is to question the whole system of constitutional monarchy. Authority, more particularly moral authority, is founded on respect. This respect does not oblige either the King's subjects or the subjects of friendly foreign governments to remain blind to blatant faults or crimes, but it obliges them to open their eyes to reality and not to refuse to recognize an error when they are in a position to check their facts.

As long as the situation remains as it is, as long as the prisoner at Laeken, by refusing to lend his support to his country's enemies, remains the centre of patriotic resistance, those who wish to dissociate him from his people cannot escape the dilemma with which they are faced. They cannot save Belgium if they wish to ruin her Sovereign. They must either try their utmost to save both or accept the heavy responsibility of ruining both.

Chapter IV

NEUTRALISM AND NEUTRALITY

ON A FINE morning, about three months ago, my
friend Samson entered my study, dropped his stick on
the floor, threw his hat on my table and flung himself
into an armchair, stretching his legs to the fire. It is
Samson's way of taking things for granted.

"Concerning your unfortunate King," he began,
"I grant you that, on the evidence which has been
produced, the accusation of treason can no longer be
maintained. I am ready to recognize that he did all in
his power to co-operate with the Allies in the defence
of his country and that the surrender of your army was
justified and unavoidable. But, to be frank with you,
I am not quite satisfied about this policy of neutrality
which he favoured so much. Why was he not at the
side of the Allies in September 1939, as his father had
been in August 1914? Even if he wished to remain
neutral during the first months of the struggle, why
did he not throw his lot with us as soon as it became
abundantly clear that Hitler had decided to invade
Belgium and Holland. Why did he even refuse to
enter into military contact with us until his country
was actually invaded? You will tell me that it is the
Law? But is it not a case where we might say that the
letter kills the spirit? I have always noticed that when
the letter of the Law is given so much importance, it is
a screen hiding something. What was it with King

Leopold? Was he afraid of Hitler, or afraid of his responsibilities? There must be something?"

1. *Clearing the air*

"Before I give you my answer," I retorted, "will you allow me to put one or two questions to you?"

"Fire away..."

"Why do you reproach his neutral attitude to King Leopold and not to the Sovereigns of other neutral nations which have not opposed the same resistance to German invasion and have suffered to a far greater extent from the activities of the Fifth Column?"

"For one thing, because we expected that they would remain neutral in this war as they had been in the last. They had some reason to rely on Germany's good faith. Your King had none. Yes, I suppose we were disappointed with Belgium because we remembered Liège and the Yser, and still more with Leopold III, because we had not forgotten Albert I. For another reason, because you stand at our very door. Lord Baldwin was right when he said that our frontier is on the Rhine. We are more immediately concerned with Belgium than with Scandinavia, for instance."

"Thank you for a candid answer. I only wished to point out, to start with, that your objection to neutrality is not merely a matter of principle. It is also a matter of expediency. It suited your purpose in 1831–1839, and was urged upon Belgium, I should say forced upon Belgium, at the time. It no longer suited your purpose in 1904, when you ceased to be the arbiter of Europe, and abandoned your "splendid isolation" to enter the Entente. The "buffer state" of the nineteenth century

93

became a "vanguard state" in the twentieth. In those days, more particularly in 1912, this question of common preparation and military conversations came to the fore, as you may remember. King Albert and his Government answered exactly as King Leopold and his Government answered in 1940. It is all very well to draw subtle distinctions between the letter and the spirit of the Law, or to say that since Hitler chose to break the Law blatantly, we should not have hesitated in turning it secretly. Shall I remind you of the negotiations pursued by the Allies with Soviet Russia before the conclusion of the Russo-German Pact? Was not that diplomatic defeat caused by your respect for the independence of the Baltic States? Could you not have bought peace at a price during these fateful weeks and squared Russia, at the expense of International Law? Events have shown that, in spite of appearances, it would not have paid the Allies to forestall Hitler's move against Holland and Belgium, but a military alliance with Russia, in August 1939, was definitely a paying proposition. The fact is that the Law remains the Law, whatever the results of its violation might be."

"In practice, this gives an enormous advantage to the law-breaker. Besides, to go back to Belgian neutrality, great changes had occurred since 1839 and 1914."

"We shall come to that. All I wish to do at present is to clear the air and dispel misunderstandings. We must agree on certain fundamental principles. The first is that there should be some rules accepted by all, or if necessary enforced upon all, the second is that these rules should be complied with, whether this compliance is profitable or not. If some of these rules, such as the right of a State to remain neutral in a conflict, have become obsolete or impracticable, they should be scrapped or altered. As long as they are not, they hold good. If one Power chooses to violate systematically international order, that is no reason why the others should follow suit. Whatever the disadvantages, the old order should be maintained by the law-abiding nations to the limit of possibilities. These disadvantages are not without compensations and the old saying that "honesty is the best policy," so frequently used by King Albert, may still come true. We heard perhaps too much, during the last war, of treaties and treaty-breaking, and the immanent power of Truth, Honour and Justice. But moral forces play, nevertheless, a very important part even in contemporary warfare. They are safely sheltered from tanks and bombs, and they are at work all the time. International Law rests on these forces and the country or the man who chooses to scorn it reaps the consequences. At one stage or another, as the struggle goes on, the world becomes divided between the supporters and the destroyers of international obligations. How are you to distinguish between them if the same methods are adopted by both sides? What we mean by Democracy is not only a democratic form of internal government, it is also a lawful relationship between states. America's change of attitude since the conflict began is a striking illustration of the power of these moral and legal forces which will ultimately tilt the balance on our side."

"Very well, I am ready to accept your fundamental

95

principles. You have still to show that they tally with King Leopold's policy which was adopted in 1936, after the Covenant, after Locarno, and which broke away from collective security."

2. *"The King's Policy"*

"To begin with, it was not the King's personal policy. It was a policy imposed upon him by the external and internal circumstances under which he was placed.

"When Hitler denounced Locarno in March 1936, the King and his Government fully realized the danger to which Belgium was exposed. Although the international situation had deteriorated during the previous years, the demilitarization of the Rhineland had hitherto remained the bulwark of Belgian security. Suddenly, this barrier disappeared and the treaty of mutual guarantee which, unlike Versailles, had been publicly accepted by the Führer, was torn up like any old scrap of paper.

"M. van Zeeland, the King's personal friend, was then at the head of the Government. He came to London to confer with the representatives of the three other great Powers (Italy had not yet joined the Axis) in order to put to them a very pertinent question: 'What do you intend to do in order to keep your word and to protect us while you protect yourselves, and with yourselves the whole civilized world?'[1]

"M. Flandin, although inclined to start military operations, does not seem to have shown great determination, owing no doubt to the fact that his Cabinet

[1] P. van Zeeland, in *The Belgian Campaign*, p. 13.

was divided on this question and that France was ill-prepared to launch an offensive. Mr. Eden remarked that British public opinion could not agree to a war which aimed at expelling German troops from German soil. The Italian delegate was still less inclined to favour military action against the Reich at a time when the Duce was growing more and more impatient at the objections raised in this country against his African ambitions. What could M. van Zeeland do?

"Belgium had concluded, in September 1920, a military convention with France which had been the subject of strong criticism among the Flemish Party. She had reluctantly followed France into the Ruhr, in 1923, and had been stigmatized in this country as a "subservient satellite" of her big neighbour. Since Locarno, it had been evident that, for national as well as for international reasons, Belgium could no longer be a party to a one-sided arrangement. The Belgian Premier declared, and we may safely assume that the Sovereign shared his views, that Belgium would adhere to any plan adopted jointly by Britain and France and would endeavour to do all in her power to bring them together if they did not agree. The result was a fatal postponement which allowed Hitler to pursue his rearmament and to detach Mussolini from the Stresa front. He had skilfully suggested a new Western Pact which became the subject of a series of fruitless proposals, while the former Locarno Powers (including Belgium) engaged in sterile staff conversations. No time limit was fixed, no definite plan drawn up.[1]

[1] Only one meeting took place in London in the spring of 1936 and no suggestion was made of any future common action.

"Remember March 1936, my friend, that is the turning point of Belgian policy. Everything which happened later is explained by this crucial meeting in London. We are all responsible for this failure, no doubt, but did you expect Belgium to give a lead to France, Great Britain and Italy? The opportunity was lost.

"Shortly afterwards, Mussolini joined the Axis, and the Spanish Civil War divided Europe into two opposite camps, the one favouring Fascism, the other Communism. The reoccupation of the Rhineland and the international tension made the Belgian position more and more precarious. Like his father, before 1914, King Leopold wished to hasten preparations. He was, under the Constitution, responsible for the country's security and had to use all the means at his disposal to strengthen her defences. This necessitated new credits and prolongation of the period of military service, which Parliament was unwilling to grant as long as the country remained a partner in Locarno, and in the arrangements concluded, in March 1936, between the Treaty Powers. Under these arrangements, she had entered into military conversations with France and England and was obliged to follow their lead. Under the Treaty, she had undertaken to defend not only her own frontiers, but also those of France. This she could do, and wished to do, as long as the Treaty implied a mutual guarantee. Now that it had been denounced by one party, Germany, without any action being taken against her, Belgian commitments became one-sided. She was, for the time being, an ally of France who followed a policy which the majority of Belgians deplored without being able to alter it. Through the Franco-Soviet pact, or other alliances concluded in Eastern or Central Europe, Belgium could at any moment be drawn into a conflict in which her interests were not directly involved. Most Belgians looked askance at the Communist agitation and the stay-in strikes which prevailed in France at the time. Remember that one of the principles of British policy in modern history, has always been to avoid commitments in Central and Eastern Europe, excepting the straits of Constantinople. Is it to be wondered at if Belgium, after waiting for six months for the conclusion of the new Western Pact, with a reoccupied Rhineland on the one side and a restless France on the other, expressed the wish to be released from her Locarno obligations?[1]

"King Leopold has been accused of being anti-French. He was neither pro- nor anti-French. He would have been actively pro-British if, by this time, British policy had not already been linked up with French policy, and if Britain had fulfilled her intention to re-arm, especially in the air.[2] But he was above all pro-Belgian and, like most of his compatriots, could only see with apprehension the way in which France took various diplomatic initiatives likely to provoke Germany's opposition, without taking adequate measures

---

[1] I might have added that, even if she had not expressed this wish, she would in no way have been obliged to enter the war in September, 1939, since the Rhine Pact only concerned Western Europe.

[2] *Cf*. Baldwin's declarations in Parliament, in November, on the unsatisfactory state of British rearmament.

to meet this opposition. Thus far, but no farther, went King Leopold's anti-French or pro-German feelings.

"To the rulers of big Powers, it seems unbelievable that the Government of a small neighbouring state should follow an independent policy. Every Belgian Sovereign, including King Albert, has been abused for his pro-French or pro-German attitude, at one time or other. But as long as this right is recognized, no reproach can be directed against the smaller States for seeking their security where they hope to find it.

"King Leopold did not embrace neutrality as an ideal. Neutrality can never be an ideal, but it certainly was at the time an urgent necessity. In Germany, re-armament proceeded very rapidly, in France and Britain it seemed constantly hampered by political or military illusions. This state of unpreparedness of the Allies rendered Belgian preparations all the more urgent. At all costs, opposition in Parliament had to be overcome. A change of policy was the only means of overcoming it. If the people were reassured on the score of entanglements, they would not refuse to make the necessary sacrifices. After the fluctuations of the big Powers' policy during the last years, any appeal based on international friendship would have been vain. The Government could only obtain the men and the money if Parliament received a guarantee that the defence of Belgium alone was concerned.

"On October 14th 1936, M. van Zeeland and his colleagues gathered in council at the Palace. The King presided and addressed his Ministers in the following terms: 'The reoccupation of the Rhineland, by altering completely the Locarno agreements . . .

has placed us again in the same international position which we held before the war' (that is, in 1914, when Belgium was neutral and Europe divided into two groups of hostile powers). 'Our geographical position compels us to maintain sufficient defensive forces to dissuade any of our neighbours from using our territory in order to attack another state. In fulfilling this mission, Belgium contributes in no mean fashion to the preservation of peace in Western Europe and obtains, *ipso facto*, the right to be respected, and eventually supported, by all states which are concerned in the preservation of peace. Within these limits, I believe that Belgian opinion will be unanimous. But no engagement should compel us to go further.'[1]

"Such deliberations are usually kept secret, but, on this special occasion, the Cabinet considered that the Sovereign's arguments, by conciliating the opponents of military reforms, particularly in Flemish quarters, would rally public opinion. At the suggestion of the veteran Socialist leader, M. Vandervelde, who could scarcely be suspected of submissiveness to the Crown, the Council unanimously asked King Leopold's permission to publish his speech. It was evidently meant for home consumption. Owing to an oversight, certain papers, while publishing it, omitted to mention the circumstances in which it was delivered, and the impression was created abroad that the views it expressed, which were really the views of the whole Cabinet in which the three main political parties were represented, were the personal views of the Sovereign. This was the beginning of a misunderstanding which was

[1] See Appendix II.

destined to cause endless harm by disassociating the King's policy from that of the Belgian people, the Belgian Parliament and the Belgian Cabinet, a misunderstanding which was exploited at home and abroad by those who disapproved of the change. A minority of Belgians combined with an increasing number of Frenchmen and Britishers to represent the 1936–1937 Belgian policy as imposed upon a reluctant nation by an autocratic monarch and a subservient Government, while it had really been determined by the unwillingness of the Belgians to make fresh sacrifices for defence if the provisory situation in which the country found herself was not modified, and her rights and duties clearly defined.

"I repeat, it was not King Leopold's personal policy, It was the policy of M. van Zeeland and, later, of M. Spaak and M. Pierlot, it was the policy of the Belgian Chamber which approved it, on October 28th, by 126 votes to 42, it was the policy of 95 per cent of the Belgian people.[1] The opposition, which included the bulk of the Flemish Nationalists and Communists and a small number of Liberal and Socialist supporters of collective security, decreased during the following years. This was shown after the crisis of 1938 and as late as April 17th 1940, three weeks before the invasion, when the Belgian Senate gave the Government an overwhelming majority on this question (131 to 3).

"It has been suggested that this change of policy was caused by fear. I believe that it was caused by the failure of the League and by the return of the world

[1] See van Zeeland in *The Belgian Campaign*.

102

to power politics. It came five years after Manchuria, one year after Abyssinia, six months after the denunciation of Locarno and the reoccupation of the Rhineland, four months after the Spanish Civil War and the policy of non-intervention. It has been suggested that it was caused by pro-Nazi tendencies. The only parties where the Nazis have found any political sympathisers, since May last, are the Flemish Nationalists and the Rexists. They belonged to the Opposition.

"Some illusions might have been entertained in Brussels, in 1936, as in London and Paris as late as 1938, concerning the possibility of conciliating Hitler, but neither the Sovereign nor the Government had exaggerated hopes on the political issue. It was precisely because they sensed the German danger that they took what they considered the only measures which might still save Belgium from becoming once more the battlefield of Europe. The Germans themselves tried to justify their action, on May 10th 1940, by pointing out that all Belgian preparations were directed towards the protection of the Eastern frontier.

"What prompted King Leopold to deliver his speech of October 1936, was neither fear, nor submissiveness. It was his sense of duty. He has been reproached for being sad and stern. He had every reason to be. To adopt Mr. Lloyd George's expression, when he denounced the King as a traitor and a coward, 'you can rummage in vain through the annals of history' to find a young constitutional Sovereign confronted, from the first days of his reign, with more pressing and anxious problems, involving the life and happiness of his people. In ascending the throne, he had promised to safeguard Belgian integrity and independence. He had also sworn to remain faithful to the Constitution. How could he comply with one promise without breaking the other? He chose the only way open to him. The League was evidently by then incapable of preventing an aggression. The Pact of Locarno had gone, and no other Pact had been concluded to replace it. A military alliance with Britain and France might have been possible, if these powers had been hastening their military preparations. But France had, for several years, embarked upon a dangerous policy in which remote or unreliable alliances took the place of reliable rearmament. She was swayed between periods of provocative self-assertion and periods of unaccountable weakness. Whatever action Britain took, it did not increase the steadiness and determination of her partner. She seemed equally anxious to avoid a conflict or to tackle decisively her own rearmament problem. The Belgian people had to be consulted and, faced by the vacillations and indecisions of Franco-British policy, the Belgian people preferred to recover their freedom of action. The strengthening of the Eastern frontier dominated the King's preoccupation. He and his Government did what they did in order to preserve national unity and to obtain sufficient support for the urgent measures rendered necessary by the reoccupation of the Rhineland. They were not prompted by patriotic motives only, but hoped that by barring the way to a new German aggression, they might either prevent it altogether or help the Allies to parry the blow directed against them."

"Nevertheless," objected Samson, "we had the impression at the time that the King, or if you prefer, the Belgian people, resumed their neutrality or their independence because they felt that Hitler was growing too strong for them."

"Evidently, he was too strong for them—alone. Whether he would have been too strong in March or October 1936, for Britain, France, Belgium, Czecho-Slovakia and perhaps Soviet Russia, is another matter. But no common action was proposed, six months after the denunciation of Locarno, and after the failure of a series of stillborn 'plans'.

"If Belgium had merely declared her intention of recovering her liberty of action without warning her old Allies, she might have been accused of ingratitude. But she had warned them repeatedly through diplomatic channels before October 1936, and only altered her policy after reaching an agreement with them through a series of negotiations lasting nearly six months. The King came himself to London to confer with Mr. Eden on this question, and Mr. Eden returned his visit in April 1937, when he went to Brussels in order to sign the final document. It was only in the following October that a similar arrangement was concluded with the Reich. If you call that letting one's friends down, you must admit that it is a gentle way of doing it."

"I have never been quite clear about this Franco-British Declaration," remarked my friend.

"That is another misfortune. Somehow, it does not seem to have attracted much attention. Nothing shows better the decadence of the prestige of Law, in modern days, than the way this agreement was forgotten as soon as it was concluded. To the Belgian people, it was a new charter, defining the country's international position, almost as important as the 1839 treaties; to the Allied people, it was only an incident in the diplomatic game which was soon to bring Europe to the verge of ruin. Who remembers the Franco-British Declaration to-day, outside the Foreign Office and a few learned Institutes? Who remembered, in September 1939, and in May 1940, that the Allies had recognized, three years before, that Belgium's desire to determine her rights and obligations was justified "in view of her geographical position and of the delays which may still ensue in the negotiation and conclusion of a general Act destined to replace the Treaty of Locarno." (France still hoped to induce Hitler to come to the conference table.) Who remembered that both Great Britain and France had released Belgium from all her previous undertakings, including the famous Staff conversations, provided she prevented Belgian territory '*from being used in case of an aggression against another State either as a passage or as a basis of operations*' by organizing 'efficiently her defences.'[1]

"The wording is important. You will notice that the new agreement put a stop to the military conversations in which Belgium was later reproached for not joining, and excluded the passage of any foreign army through Belgian territory which Belgium was later reproached for not permitting.

"The whole document shows that the Allies understood perfectly well that it was in their own interest, as well as in that of Belgium, that the country should

[1] See Appendix III.

106

remain united and should devote herself to the organization of her defences. Had they thought otherwise,
they would have said so then and there, and would
have washed their hands of the consequences if Belgium, invoking the principle of national sovereignty,
had chosen to remain alone, facing the common
danger. But they did not. They almost gave the new
policy their diplomatic blessing, generously recognized
the validity of the motives which prompted it and,
what is still more significant, maintained their military
guarantee.

"One of the main reasons, on the Belgian side, for
pursuing these negotiations was to avoid any misunderstanding arising, in case of conflict, from her
decision to observe neutrality and to remain faithful to
her obligations as a neutral.[1] The Belgian negotiators
had foreseen everything in preparing this document,
except that it should be entirely ignored when the
conflict began, so that the Belgians would be repeatedly criticized for having done what they had said they
would do, and for remaining faithful to an undertaking
countersigned by the representatives of the British and
French Governments.

"Again and again, in 1940, Belgian neutrality was
denounced and derided in this country as betraying a
weakness of purpose and an anxiety to pacify Hitler and
all he stands for. Again and again, when I alluded to

[1] *Cf.* M. Spaak's speech of April 16th 1940: "Few countries
have succeeded better than we have in defining their aims,
limiting their engagements . . . , enlightening their neighbours
on their intentions. . . . *Whatever happens, no one will be able to
say that he has been betrayed by Belgium.*"

the 1937 Franco-British Declaration, I realized that it had lost all real significance. It belonged to past history. I might just as well have spoken of the 1839 treaties. What was justified and reasonable in 1937 became absurd and somewhat suspicious in 1940.

"Must we recognize that, since Hitler chose to violate neutrality, neutrality no longer exists, that because the Law has been broken, Law has lost all meaning? Do you realize that every criticism directed against neutrality in 1940 might have been made in 1912–1914, when military conversations had been discouraged by King Albert and his Government, as they were, last year, by King Leopold and his Government? What will happen to small nations if this ruthless spirit prevails at the end of hostilities?"

3. *Collective Security*

"You may well ask," replied Samson. "I am afraid jurists will have a poor time of it. You see, International Law was all very well in the old days when wars only concerned the monarchs and their small armies. But the democratisation of international conflicts has revolutionized the old system of contractual obligations to which you seem to cling so desperately. The rights and duties of Neutrals have gone the same way as the Laws and Usages of warfare. These old customs may still be observed by the overscrupulous, as long as they do not stand too much in the way. They have lost all meaning for the others, unless they serve to camouflage some aggressive project or to lull suspicions. You talk as if the world had developed on the same lines from 1918 to 1940 as from 1839 to 1914, as if we had had no League of Nations, no collective security. You are making a very grave mistake."

I referred Samson to Professor Carr's shrewd analysis of the "Twenty Years' Crisis." I reminded him how and why the League had failed to apply sanctions against the aggressor before 1937 in Manchuria, the Gran Chaco, Abyssinia and Spain, and of the rapid disintegration of collective security which the series of successful challenges to the new order provoked.

"When we signed the Declaration," I added, "the new system fostered by the League had already become so weak that we had to go back to the old system of balance of power and neutrality. We were accused of 'giving the death blow to collective security'. No action of Belgium, could have obtained such sweeping results. Collective security was dead long before and, in spite of Mr. Stimson's declarations after the signature of the Kellogg Pact, neutrality had never been completely obsolete. Switzerland had made it a condition of her joining the League, to be exempted from allowing League troops to cross her territory. Article XVI of the Covenant, concerning military co-operation, was the subject of strong reservations, in favour of Germany, when the latter signed the Locarno treaty in 1925. She was only bound to act 'to an extent compatible with her military situation' and her 'geographical position'. Attention had been drawn on several occasions, in the Parliaments of the small Western States, to the fact that, since the big Powers refused to apply sanctions, the small Powers might consider the military clauses of the Covenant as purely optional. On July 1st 1936, that is to say three months before King Leopold's speech, the Ministers of Foreign Affairs of Denmark, Spain, Norway, Holland, Sweden and Switzerland issued, in Geneva, a formal statement to the effect that 'as long as the Covenant was only applied incompletely . . . they were obliged to take this fact into account in their interpretation of Article XVI'.

"Neutrality was the necessary consequence of the failure of sanctions. Belgium was not the first but the last small Western State to return to it, if you choose to give this meaning to her change of policy. The last doubt disappeared on the eve of the September crisis of 1938, when a British declaration on the optional character of Article XVI was followed by a joint statement of the members of the Oslo group, confirming their decision to remain neutral in case of conflict. By the beginning of the present war, the legality of neutrality and its compatibility with League membership were no longer questioned."

"Strange," exclaimed Samson, "that a lawyer like myself should not be entirely satisfied by such arguments. If we discussed Civil Law it would be different. Your position would be safe enough. But in international affairs, you must take into account the psychological element. In answer to my objection concerning the antiquated system of balance of power and neutrality, you tell me that it had not been replaced by anything valid. I agree, but it had been nevertheless destroyed. People had ceased to believe in it. It had no longer any solid foundations. We had demolished the old house and erected a ramshackle building in its place. The new structure soon came to grief, but the old one was not restored. Nothing was done. We groped among heaps of ruins. Every wall we touched gave way. I agree with Professor Carr about the danger of utopia. The tragedy is that you cannot go back when it has led you astray. By that time, the centre of gravity of the world has shifted, so that your solution is neither the old one, nor the one which has just been found wanting, but a third one which lies between the two. I do not say that the views of King Leopold—or if you prefer, of the Belgian people—were not sound when they left Locarno, and I recognize that we had nothing better to offer them than another spell of 'wait and see,' but I do say that, after our recent experience, neutrality has indeed become obsolete. It might have rendered great services when International Law enjoyed a certain prestige. It is positively dangerous to-day. For instance, it prevented you from taking decisive steps towards our common defence when the danger of Belgian invasion became evident."

4. *Alliance in extremis?*

"I do not wish to score points," I replied, "but you will notice that the more we consider this business of neutrality, the more we realize that it looks different in 1936, in 1939, and, more particularly, in 1940. What is perfectly legitimate before the war becomes almost intolerable during the war. Even during the first months of the conflict the position of neutral

111

Italy or of neutral Peru was far more favourable than that of neutral Belgium. It all depends on circumstances, power, size and geographical situation.[1]

"As for engaging in secret preparations with the Allies as soon as the immediate danger became evident, may I point out to you that, besides being a breach of law, such a move was practically impossible in a democratic country where foreign journalists must be allowed to carry on their work. The secret would have leaked out and placed in the hands of the would-be aggressor an excellent excuse for violating his pledge. Belgium would have had the Law as well as the big battalions against her.

"You are always speaking of Belgium and the Allies but you do not take sufficiently into consideration the relationship between the Belgian King and Government and the Belgian people. Once the war started, once neutrality proclaimed on the Belgian side and promises given by all the belligerents that it would be respected, how could the Sovereign or his Ministers take the responsibility of doing anything involving such a risk? Solemn pledges had been exchanged in 1936 between the Government and the people. Men and money had been given by the latter against non-commitment and neutrality from the former. After the Declaration of 1937 and the policy followed in September 1938 and 1939, there was no longer any change possible. Belgium had tried collective security under the League and regional alliances under

[1] I could not foresee, when this conversation took place, that Yugoslavia's proclamation of neutrality, in March 1941, would have been rightly considered as nothing short of heroic.

112

Locarno, she had to follow the last road open to her and remain faithful to her undertakings."

"King Leopold seems to have been particularly persistent in following it," remarked Samson.

"I suppose you are alluding to the appeals made in August and November 1939? They concern, not only Belgium but all the small Western States and more particularly Holland who was faced with the same problem and tried to solve it in a similar way. Remember that when we are dealing with neutrality, we are dealing with all these States and that, if Belgium and her Government committed an error, these States and their Governments committed the same error.

"Yes, King Leopold wished to do his utmost first to prevent war and, later, to prevent the invasion of his country, but this was also the wish of Queen Wilhelmina and the other neutral Sovereigns. On the eve of the conflict, on August 23rd 1939, the Belgians took the initiative of inviting the Ministers for Foreign Affairs of the Western neutral States to come to Brussels. At the close of the meeting, King Leopold was asked by the delegates to broadcast an appeal, which he did, in his own name and in those of the Heads of the seven other States represented at the Conference. I have it here: 'The small countries are faced with the fear of a conflict into which they might be dragged, in spite of their will to retain their neutrality. . . . We want peace with respect for all nations. . . . To-morrow hundreds of millions of people will be hoping that the differences which separate Heads of States may be settled by means of conciliation. Let those in whose hands rests the destiny of these peoples apply themselves to settle peacefully the differences which separate them."[1]

"How futile!" exploded Samson, "think of Hitler reading that!"

"If it was futile, the futility was shared by a good many people. There was certainly nothing personal about it. As for Hitler, he would only have benefited from the policy of conciliation advocated in the appeal in so far as it prevented the Allies or the neutrals from making the necessary military preparations. Belgium had done more than any other Western State to strengthen her defences. It is perhaps the reason why she has been so often depicted as the weakest and most deluded victim of Nazism.

"A second step was taken on August 28th, when it had been made clear that the first appeal would receive no answer. Both M. Pierlot, in Brussels, and M. van Kleffens, at the Hague, invited the representatives of the Powers in the Belgian and Dutch capitals, and told them that the Queen of Holland and the King of the Belgians were prepared 'jointly to lend their good offices' towards possible negotiations.

"This, once more, failed, and the difficulties of practical neutrality, connected with economic and air warfare began. There were two serious scares before the final catastrophe. A few weeks after the end of the Polish campaign, late in October, the Dutch received certain information pointing at an early attack on their Eastern frontier. The Foreign Minister advised the Queen to make an attempt at mediation, and she communicated at once with Brussels. King

[1] See Appendix VIII.

Leopold and M. Spaak arrived late the same evening (November 5th). The fact that General van Overstraeten, the King's military adviser, accompanied them, is significant. There was no time to lose since the intended attack was supposed to take place on the 12th. The next day, the offer was sent to the King of England, the President of the French Republic and the German Chancellor. It was more pressing than the first: 'At this hour of anxiety for the whole world, before the war breaks out in Western Europe . . . we have the conviction that it is our duty once again to raise our voice. Some time ago the belligerent parties declared that they would not be unwilling to examine a reasonable and well founded basis for an equitable peace. . . . As Sovereigns of two neutral States having good relations with all their neighbours, we are ready to offer them our good offices. . . . This, it seems to us, is the task we have to fulfil for the good of our people and in the interests of the whole world."

"You may remember that this flying visit of King Leopold was misinterpreted and that, after the surrender of his army it was suggested that, being scared by some false news, he rushed to the Hague in order to obtain Queen Wilhelmina's moral and diplomatic support . . ."[1]

"What I am trying to get at," interrupted Samson, "is whether there was no moment when it might have been possible for Belgium or Holland to join the Allies, since they knew perfectly well that Hitler's actions were purely determined by 'military necessities'. They were not obliged to remain neutral. They might have

[1] *Cf.* note p. 84.

115

found excellent reasons, the invasion of Norway, for instance."

"Here is the explanation given by M. van Kleffens in *The Rape of the Netherlands*: 'Once Germany had invaded Holland, voices in other countries were not lacking which contended that, if only Holland had entered into some defensive arrangement with the Allies in time, she would not have suffered the fate the German attack brought upon her. This argument seems altogether futile. There is not the slightest doubt that, the moment Germany had learnt (and heaven knows her intelligence service is ubiquitous) that the Dutch Government was plotting with the Allies, she would have attacked at once, long before the Allies could have sent any troops to our assistance.' Replace Dutch by Belgian in every sentence, and this is my answer. Once the war had begun it was too late. The pledge given to the people had to be kept, and no public debate on the subject was possible. Besides, in the light of what happened later, can you still maintain that such a move would have considerably altered the military position?"

"Forgive me for driving you so hard," insisted Samson, "but, after all, your aim is to vindicate King Leopold's reputation and, personally, I am convinced that M. Reynaud's suggestions would not have been accepted so readily in this country if we had not been prejudiced against your King on account of this very question of neutrality. There were other neutrals and other surrenders, but the combination of neutralism and capitulation, in one and the same person, proved too much for popular imagination."

116

"What exactly do you wish to know? You have recognized that, in spite of our efforts to remain at the side of the Allies, we were driven back upon neutrality by events beyond our control. When could the King and his Government—do not forget that they always worked together in the closest co-operation—take this tremendous decision of plunging their small country into the most destructive of all wars? In November 1939, when the Dutch were threatened? In the following January, when we had another severe scare, after the landing of a German plane and the discovery of certain German military plans? None of these scares proved justified. The Dutch intelligence service might have been at fault, in November. The documents seized at Mechelen, in January, might have been faked. We had two or three other alerts which were never mentioned, and there is good reason to believe that the order of invasion was more than once cancelled at the eleventh hour. There is no certainty in such matters and, after the pledges given in Parliament,[1] no action could possibly be taken without absolute certainty.

"The Government's difficulties were aggravated, on several occasions, by certain steps taken by the French who were kept informed of all important developments. Not for one moment did the Belgians imagine that these steps might lead to military action, but they placed them in a false position and might have provided Hitler with a suitable pretext. But I must be discreet and will only read to you this extract from

[1] In April, 1937, M. Spaak had declared that there only remained one possible reason for war, namely "national defence".

Elie Bois' last book: 'As regards Belgium, the Allies were not in a very happy position. Repeatedly since the beginning of the war they had sounded the Chancellery of Brussels with the object of inducing the Belgian Government to appeal for Franco-British intervention before the German invasion became an accomplished fact. Each time, the request was refused on the ground that the slightest gesture might furnish a pretext for violation by Germany of Belgian neutrality and that, as long as that neutrality was not violated it had the advantage for France of preventing the Maginot Line being turned. . . . Was there not a risk in making another diplomatic advance, doomed to failure like the previous ones, of producing an unfortunate impression in Brussels? . . . M. Paul Reynaud did not think so. *Against the formal advice of his diplomatic counsellors he raised the matter with the Supreme Council and got the better of British hesitation.* . . . Barely had the request been made during one night, when the negative response was returned immediate and categorical. . . . This lack of care over the form of action and the choice of the moment is an indication of the state of physical and mental inferiority in which disappointments, illness and fear of political disgrace had brought M. Paul Reynaud.'[1]

"What the Belgians could do, and what they did in January, in spite of repeated German protests, was to transfer all their troops to the East, leaving their

[1] *The Truth about the Tragedy of France.* In his recent book, *Seven Mysteries of Europe*, M. Jules Romains tells us that he went to Brussels, in October 1939, on a self-appointed mission, in order "to force the King to reveal his real feelings and to state where he stood."

Southern frontier unguarded, and to provide the French Command with all the information required to facilitate co-operation after the aggression had taken place.[1] What they also did was to work in close connection with their Northern neighbours. It would take too long to explain to you why the plan of a defensive alliance with the Dutch never materialized. It would not have been inconsistent with the 1936–1937 policy, but met with considerable practical difficulties on account of the nature of the Dutch defensive plans and of the geographical configuration of the two countries. Remember also that the transition from collective security to power politics had been too short to allow the small states sufficient time to adapt themselves to the new situation.

"During the crisis of November 1939, the question of military collaboration had been raised. It had been remarked that if the Belgians interfered on a large scale, were Holland to be invaded, their own defences would be considerably weakened. The Government and the King considered nevertheless that an attack on central Holland, by turning the Belgian defences, would constitute a direct threat to Belgian security. Common danger had brought the two peoples closer together, and M. Spaak met with no opposition when he declared, on December 19th, that 'although he

[1] This is a conclusive answer to the accusation that they attached the same value to German and French promises. On February 7th 1940, General Denis declared in Parliament that the Belgian authorities would neglect nothing to enable the guarantor Powers to discharge their obligations. In answer to an enquiry, the Generalissimo assured the Belgian High Command that he had received all the information he required.

preferred to remain entirely free and not to come to a solution before knowing all the elements of the problem,' he wished to state 'firmly that it would be extremely foolish to proclaim that a change in the situation of Holland could leave Belgium indifferent.' A similar statement was made before the Senate a few weeks before the invasion. It was duly appreciated at the time in the Allied Press, but, as many other things, it is almost forgotten to-day.

"I forgive you for driving me hard, my friend, but if you wish to be fair you should practice the art of looking at a thing from both points of view. I quite realize that as a Britisher, you should smile condescendingly at these weak efforts of Belgium at asserting herself. Britain has the whole Empire at her back, the strongest Fleet in the world, and if not the largest at any rate the best Air Force. Now, take my place, look at Belgium. She can be overrun in a week, transformed within a few days from a happy and prosperous country into a desolate battlefield. We could not evacuate our population from the danger zone along the Eastern frontier, as the French did behind the Maginot Line. There was no room available. The country is overcrowded even in normal circumstances. These are perhaps only material considerations, but such considerations cannot be ignored by those who assume the responsibility of Government. As long as there was the faintest hope, the faintest chance, they had no right to take the plunge. Call it fear, if you like, this fear is not selfish, there is no dishonour in being afraid of betraying a sacred trust."

"I expect," remarked Samson, "that our present

prejudice against neutrality rests on the conviction that
we are so much in the right, in this quarrel, and that
the other side is so much in the wrong. We feel that
all right-minded people should have joined us."

"The question is, when? In 1937, when the French
still hoped against hope to negotiate a new Western
Pact with Hitler? In 1938, when Britain and France
reached an agreement with him and allowed him to
break it six months later? In September 1939? It was
too late. A great Power can convert appeasement into
resistance, if public opinion is sufficiently roused. A
small state cannot convert neutrality into an alliance
involving immediate hostilities, because public opinion
will never accept such a decision. There is a big-power
complex inclining the worst of them to sheer brutality
and the best of them to pugnacity, and a small-power
complex inclining the worst of them to subservience
and the best of them to cautiousness. We had to ex-
haust all the possibilities afforded by the attitude we
had chosen. We had to go to the end concerning
neutrality as we had gone to the end with regard to
the League and Locarno."

"It has been a bitter lesson for you", remarked
Samson, "but I admit that a sudden change, once
hostilities had started, was a practical impossibility.
Neither is there, as far as I can see, any connection
between the Belgian military tragedy of May 1940,
and the diplomatic change heralded by King Leopold's
speech in 1936. What we British feel rather strongly
is that the whole thing works against us, that we are
placed at a disadvantage in our struggle against the
Nazis owing to a system which forbids the victim of

aggression to join its defenders and the defender to forestall their enemy's intentions. This is particularly aggravating when the victims must be aware of the fact that one of our war aims is to save them from these aggressions. Well, since we are told now to look ahead and not to look back, I promise not to mention the subject any more. We have done with neutrality, and I hope that Belgium has done with it too."

Saying these words, Samson picked up his hat and stick and made for the door. I stopped him.

"One moment, my friend. I am quite ready to discard the system if you wish. But, as the smaller man of the two, I am particularly interested that you should not do so before realizing exactly why it failed."

"Because it is obsolete, of course."

"Was the League or collective security obsolete?"

"Not exactly."

"Very well, then. Neutrality failed because it was tried and found wanting, first in 1914 and later in 1940. Collective security, under the League, failed because it was never tried, it could not even be tried. What is the conclusion? If, instead of quarrelling over reparations, France and Britain had maintained their military supremacy, the "twenty years' holiday" might have lasted for ever. The prestige of Law depends on its strong arm. You need not worry your head about an international force. We, small States, have been crying for a lead for the last fifteen years. We are following it now. We shall not grumble when it is maintained, after the war, but on one condition. . . ."

"What is it?"

"Let it be strong, and let it last."

Chapter V

THE KING IN COMMAND

WHEN APPRECIATING the part played by the Sovereign in Belgium, the historian must take into account the Constitution and the usages developed by tradition, since the foundation of the independent kingdom in 1831. Bearing these in mind, he will realize that, besides the power to "warn and to advise" in all matters, the Belgian monarchs have always enjoyed a certain influence in the administration of foreign affairs and a larger influence in military questions. To put it in another way, if they cannot determine the decisions of their Government in internal affairs, they can exert a certain action in all matters concerning national defence and security. This is only the logical consequence of a system according to which the Sovereign is considered as the country's protector and defender, and as such assumes the leadership of the national army in wartime.

I have tried to explain, in a previous chapter, the motives which led King Leopold to take the initiative, in October 1936, and to support the policy of his Government in the negotiations which led to the Franco-British Declaration of April 1937. I must now give an account of the manner in which the country, under his guidance, fulfilled her duty under this agreement and resisted the aggression of Germany during the eighteen days' campaign.

The legend meets me at the start. A number of
hostile rumours began to spread around the problem of
Belgian defences from the moment when the country
assumed an independent attitude. Most of them
originated in French military circles where it was frequently said that "King Leopold had deliberately left
the French Alliance" in order to comply with Hitler's
demands. Whether the critics alluded to the Military
Convention of 1920 or the Staff Conversations of
March 1937, was never made clear. Neither the first
nor the second could be properly called an alliance.

1. *Preparations*

Since May 28th 1940, King Leopold has been
accused of committing every possible crime, but some
severe criticisms had already been directed against him
several years before. The surrender gave them a new
impetus and a fresh virulence.

Take, for instance, the mythical prolongation of the
Maginot Line along the Belgian frontier which appeared and disappeared in turn from the news since
the beginning of hostilities. It has been said that it
was "as strong" or "almost as strong" as the rest.
Those who doubted these statements suggested darkly
that the building of this section of the line had been
opposed by the Belgians who did not wish the French
Army to stay on these positions if and when the Germans invaded their own country.[1] This story was re-

[1] See, among others, G. Waterfield: *What Happened to
France*, p. 22. "The French had intended to continue the Line
. . . of strong fortifications northwards, but the Belgian Government had stated that they would consider it an unfriendly act,
so that only a weak line was built."

peated in this country during the first months of the war and elaborately embroidered upon after Holland and Belgium had been invaded. King Leopold, we were told, had "prevented the French from completing their defensive system". He should therefore bear the responsibility of their defeat. Later, after the surrender, it was explained that the reason for the King's opposition was not his desire to see the French defend Belgian territory, but his wish to allow the Germans to find no obstacle in their triumphant progress towards Paris. He had always been ready to "sell the pass". In the excitement which prevailed at the time, it was no use pointing out that, particularly in military affairs, Paris had never been inclined to follow the dictates of Brussels and that, supposing the Belgians had raised some objections, these would promptly have been brushed aside.[1]

We know now that the "Maginot" had never been completed, in spite of the urgent advice given by the British War Office. It remained to the last a weak and straggling line of pill-boxes, either because the work was considered too costly or because the French Command wished to "keep a door open towards the North," in the hope of carrying the war into foreign territory. What has not been made sufficiently clear is that the Belgians had been just as insistent as Mr. Hore-Belisha in urging the French to complete their defensive system.

[1] We need scarcely consider here the suggestion made recently by several critics that the line which the French proposed to build "ran across Belgian territory." Such a proposal could never have been accepted by the Belgian people, but it was never made.

After the construction of the barrier along the French Eastern frontier, Belgium approached France through diplomatic and other channels, and suggested several times that the prolongation of the fortifications on the Northern frontier would provide an invaluable guarantee of security for both countries. The following communiqué was issued, on October 31st 1936, by the Belgian official agency, with the approval of the Quai d'Orsay: "In 1932, Baron de Gaiffier d'Hestroy, Belgian Ambassador in Paris, was instructed by his Government to make known to French official quarters that Belgium would be glad to see France fortify her Northern frontier and, by so doing, materially and morally strengthen the defence of Belgian national territory against any attack from the East." On November 7th 1933, M. de Tessand, Under-Secretary of State at the Ministry of Foreign Affairs, was approached officially and, the same year, M. Daladier, General Gamelin and M. Messimy, President of the Senate Military Commission, were also sounded on the subject. Ever since, the Belgian Government had considered that the non-completion of the Maginot Line considerably increased the risk of invasion, as the fortified works erected by Belgium on her Eastern frontier could not compete with the great French concrete rampart. As a first line, they should have proved efficient, but they were never intended to withstand successfully a main attack.

In this matter, as in all others, King Leopold pursued the policy initiated by his father. Before 1936, and even after that date, while speeding up Belgian preparations, he did all in his power to draw the Allies' attention to the danger of delay and procrastination. His main source of anxiety was the reluctance shown by them to make the necessary sacrifices, while the German armaments increased by leaps and bounds. His knowledge of the situation, without in the least deterring him from the resolution he had taken—to defend the country to the last if attacked—prompted him to use every means available, first to prevent the outbreak of war and, later, to prevent its extension to the West. The Belgo-Dutch offers of mediation, for instance, should be considered in connection with French military unpreparedness.

This state of unpreparedness has been shown by events. The wildest illusions prevailed, nevertheless, on the subject in August 1939 and April 1940, and those who raised an awkward question were strongly suspected of being anti-French.

Leaving the domain of myth and entering that of reality I should, before proceeding with our story, give a few facts showing how far Belgium, and with her King Leopold, fulfilled the pledges they had given to the Allies in 1937.

In the Franco-British Declaration, Belgium had undertaken (*a*) to defend her territory against aggression or against any attempts, from a foreign power, to send troops through it or to establish in it bases of operation, and (*b*) to organize efficiently the country's defence. The new policy of non-commitment should be judged by its results. If Belgian defences were placed on a proper footing, if the necessary sacrifices were made, neither Belgium nor her King can be reproached for having failed in their obligations. If, on the other hand, the promise to prepare against an attack, and to defend themselves when attacked, was merely a means used by the King and his Government to obtain the approval of the Allies for their new policy, then they might be accused of weakness or even disloyalty, since by not fulfilling their promise they exposed those who trusted them to an unforeseen danger.

The military reforms voted by Parliament in December 1936, on the strength of the Government's change of policy, increased ordinary expenses from 766 million to 1,146 million francs. The period of military service was lengthened to seventeen months and the number of men and officers actually serving raised from 67,700 in 1935, to 90,000 in 1938. The defensive works begun in the reign of King Albert were actively pursued. A first line of small fortified positions was completed along the Eastern frontier; behind it, ran a stronger line, in front of Liège, which was prolonged by the Albert Canal. Work was also planned on the Antwerp-Namur line which had played an important part in August 1914. Both Liège and Namur were considerably strengthened and their armament modernized. Owing partly to the fact that an attack upon Holland had to be foreseen, Antwerp could no longer be considered as the last refuge of the Belgian Army. The line of retreat pointed southwards but every one believed that, if the worst came to the worst, with an army "ten times stronger", Belgium, with the help of the Allies, could this time stop the invader either on the Meuse, or at least in front of Brussels.

During the following years, the Belgian Government devoted to defence no less than 10 to 12 per cent of the total expenses of the State, this proportion rising to 24 per cent after September 1939.[1] A year before, a partial mobilization had allowed the Belgian Staff to place 300,000 men on the Eastern frontier. After the outbreak of war, the forces manning the Belgian defences grew rapidly to 500,000 and, later, 600,000. Thanks to financial sacrifices entailing drastic taxation, the country had succeeded in raising an army representing almost 10 per cent of her total population.[2] A corresponding effort in Great Britain alone would have provided this country, in 1939, with a force of 4,000,000 men.

Unfortunately, in modern warfare, the machine counts for more than numbers. The Belgians were not unaware of the fact and had taken great trouble to equip their 22 infantry divisions, 2 "cavalry" divisions (motorized) and 1 armoured brigade. Nevertheless, it seems to-day that a smaller force, more strongly armed and supported from the air, would have opposed a greater resistance to the enemy. Once more—as in 1914 with her heavy Skoda siege guns—Germany succeeded in surprising her opponents. The Allies lacked planes and tanks, but nowhere was this shortage felt more sorely than on the Belgian front. There were about 250 first-line Belgian planes available at the beginning of hostilities, most of them out of date. A certain number were destroyed on the ground at the

[1] 9% in 1936, 11.3% in 1937, 11.12% in 1938.
[2] Including the reserve and the men in training; 46% of the men between 20 and 40 years of age were mobilized.

start. After the retreat to the Scheldt, German mastery of the air became unchallenged, the R.A.F. being too much engaged on the British front to be able to give any help.

This is perhaps the main reproach which might be made to King Leopold and his advisers. It seems never to have been mentioned. With better reason than the French, considering the limited resources of the country, the Belgians might plead that they could not face the expenses entailed by the purchase of aircraft from abroad and that, besides, these had become unobtainable. They might add that the proximity of the German frontier rendered the establishment of air-bases in Belgian territory precarious, and that they had to rely, in this respect, on their guarantors' help. The fact remains that, like their Allies, they did not foresee that the air-arm and the tanks would dominate operations to such a vast extent. Thanks to the *Luftwaffe*, the enemy succeeded in overcoming most of the obstacles accumulated in its path in the way of light fortifications, anti-tank traps, land mines, etc. . . . German methods did not prevail in the same way against the forts of Liège and Namur. They might have failed in front of the strong fortified works of the Antwerp-Namur line if the Belgians and the Allies had had the chance of defending them.

To sum up, although the promise given in April 1937, was kept in the spirit and in the letter, the Belgian Command, relying on a defensive action, had not provided the army with all the equipment necessary in a war of movement. This does not alter the fact that the surprise attack carried out by the *Blitz* might have been overcome and checked if a continuous front had been maintained. The break-through at Sedan is the direct cause of the retreat upon the Scheldt and of the defeat and surrender of the Belgian army. Its deficiency in aircraft and heavy tanks would not have had the same influence if it had not been combined with a war of movement which dislodged its divisions from strong positions prepared beforehand.

2. *The Appeal and the Plan*

It is not my purpose to give here a detailed account of the eighteen days' campaign through Belgium. There are, however, a few facts which must be brought forward and a few legends which must be dispelled, before the part played by the Belgians in the military operations can be properly appreciated.

I have already shown that the "appeal" made by King Leopold to the guarantor Powers was only the normal result of the diplomatic relations existing between Belgium and the Allies, nothing more, nothing less.[1] In the light of subsequent events, the German offensive was bound to achieve a certain success, owing to air supremacy and other circumstances, but it would not have been such a sweeping one if the Allies' strategy had not been at fault. The French had supreme command of the operations. As soon as they suffered serious reverses, their propaganda began to hint that they were not responsible for them. It was "the Belgians' fault", as early as May 12th. It soon became "King Leopold's fault".

[1] See p. 2.

In his indictment, M. Reynaud speaks of a plan of operations, to be applied in case Belgium should be invaded, which had been prepared as early as December 1939. This declaration is more than confirmed by General Gamelin's Order of the Day, issued on May 11th 1940: "The attack which we expected since October has started this morning."

"This time, at least," wrote *The Times*, on the same day, "there has been no strategic surprise. The armies of Holland and Belgium and those of the Allies in North-Eastern France have been preparing and maturing their plans. All of them were standing yesterday morning in a state of readiness, so that a sentence, perhaps only a code word on the telephone, will have sufficed to set the machinery in motion."

All this did not prevent King Leopold's critics from saying afterwards that his refusal to enter into military conversations had wrecked the Allies' plans and that it was entirely due to him that the operations "improvised" by the Allies, in answer to his "anguished appeal," ended in disaster. This suggestion runs through M. Reynaud's indictment. It is further developed in *The Times*, on May 29th, on the morrow of the surrender: . . . "Fear is an ill counsellor, and those who are free of it themselves may suffer most from the endeavours to befriend the timid. The fears of Nazi power entertained by the neutral Belgian Government made them refuse, before the invasion, to concert plans for their defence with the Allies, though they must have foreseen as clearly as we the probability of unprovoked attack. Nevertheless, when the assault was actually delivered, they appealed at once to Great Britain and

France for help, and we could do no other than accord it instantly, and endeavour to *extemporize* for Belgium a defence that might have been systematically planned."

If *The Times* indulged in such inconsistencies, the comments made by less responsible journals may be easily imagined.

Why then, following this well-prepared plan, did the Allies go so far and so fast, without making proper preparations against a break-through? Because they wished to join the Dutch in Zeeland or the Belgians on the Albert Canal? No doubt, such an idea must have been popular with the men, but the High Command and the Government had other preoccupations. M. Reynaud was all out for sensational results and it seems that General Gamelin, pressed by his Prime Minister, felt less reluctant to take the offensive in the North than in the East. It would carry the war into Belgian territory and spare the Pas de Calais and other industrial districts the destructions suffered twenty-five years before. I have already pointed out that this may be one of the reasons why, in spite of Belgian and British warning, the Maginot was never completed.

"A choice of two plans presented itself," writes M. Elie Bois, "to accept the enemy's challenge and hurry to meet him in order to beat him back, or hold him in check; risk of a great victory, risk of a great defeat. Alternately, to allow him almost free rein in Belgium and await him in force on a defensive line, continuing from the Maginot Line and based on the great river arteries of the Scheldt and the Meuse. This was a provisional plan of prudence. The High Command decided in favour of the risks. So did the Government."

When these plans are published, M. Elie Bois's suggestion will no doubt be confirmed. In any case, the Belgian Commander-in-Chief cannot be made responsible for projects which he was not in a position to discuss. The King has been constantly upbraided for refusing to join in military conversations. He cannot, at the same time, be abused for having urged the decision taken at the time. An eloquent silence is a figure of speech, not a reality.

Another rumour which should be disposed of before we turn our attention on the campaign itself, concerns the traffic difficulties which the Allies are supposed to have experienced after they entered Belgium, owing to defeatism or inefficiency in high quarters. The best answer to these stories is the quick progress of the Allied armies. On May 10th in the afternoon, some British divisions were already east of Brussels. The same day (the first of hostilities) the French reached Gemappes and the surroundings of Namur.[1] It is scarcely believable that troops could move as speedily along "overcrowded roads".

"The roads by which we go," writes J. L. Hodson, in *Through the Dark Night*, " is marked with sticks on which is painted a black upright arrow rather resembling a plane in flight. Within two or three hours of our entry into Belgium, roads were marked as clearly and traffic guided as efficiently as at the Aldershot Tattoo." And further: "So far our own

[1] "Strategicus": *The War for World Power*, p. 251.

plan which we have put into effect has gone like clockwork and continues to go like clockwork." [1]

Statements from such eye-witnesses began only to appear in this country months after the event. By that time, the legend had thrown deep roots and flourished on misunderstandings. For there were certainly days when the constant flow of refugees hampered military movements. This was during the retreat, ordered on the 15th, not during the advance. This retreat could not be foreseen and neither the Belgians nor the British could be made responsible for it.

Had Ribbentrop known of the Allied rapid progress into Belgium when he tried to justify Nazi aggression, he would not have failed to add traffic facilities to his list of Belgian "breaches of neutrality." As a matter of fact, if the Belgians refused to enter into any plan directed against Germany, before their frontiers had been violated, they did not refuse to give some information which facilitated the progress of Allied armies through Belgian territory after this violation had taken place. [2]

3. *"As did my Father, in* 1914"

Broadcasting to America, on October 28th 1939, King Leopold, after explaining the reasons which had led the Belgian people to remain neutral in the war, gave a very clear warning to Germany: "Twenty-five years ago exactly, the Belgian Army, under my father King Albert, put a stop to the progress of a cruel invasion. If we were attacked—God preserve us from it— in spite of the solemn and categorical engagements

[1] In most cases, positions were occupied 12 hours ahead of schedule time.

[2] See note, p. 119.

given us in 1937 and renewed on the eve of the war—
we should fight without hesitation, this time with
means ten times stronger, and once more the whole
country would be found behind the Army."[1]

The Sovereign thus renewed the promise made to
the Allies, two years before, which justified and
explained his neutral attitude. He had adopted the
policy of 1936–1937 in order to obtain the means of
defence which he so sorely needed. His good faith
should be judged by results. If he allowed Belgium to
be used as a base or a passage by the Reich, the
negotiations leading to the Declaration deserved everything which has been said against it. If he did not,
the Belgian change of attitude in 1936 was vindicated,
not only by the military effort realized since, but by
the use made of these resources against the aggressor.

On May 10th 1940, King Leopold's voice was heard
once more:—

"Belgians! For the second time in a quarter of a
century, Belgium, loyal and neutral, has been attacked
by the German Empire. In spite of the most solemn
engagements signed before all the world. The Belgian
people, fundamentally peace-loving, have done all in
their power to avoid war, but between sacrifice and
dishonour, the Belgian of 1940 hesitates no less than
did the Belgian of 1914. . . . I remain faithful to my
constitutional oath, to maintain the independence and
integrity of the country. As did my father in 1914, I
have placed myself at the head of our army, with the
same faith, the same consciousness. Belgium's cause is
pure. With God's help, she will triumph."[2]

[1] Appendix IX.   [2] Appendix X.

The promise was kept.

Had success followed, or even a long, drawn-out struggle like that of the last war, people would have forgotten their gibes at Belgium's vain attempts at stopping a conflict which could not be stopped or at offering a mediation which could not be accepted. They would have realized that if, at the outbreak of hostilities, big Powers (like Italy and the United States) could claim the right of remaining neutral, the same right could not decently be refused to small ones. They would have kept silent concerning the unpleasant things they had heard about King Leopold, and hailed him as the "worthy son of a worthy sire". They would have felt disposed to regret their jokes about the trembling little fellow trying vainly to pacify the ogre, seeing that, when the crucial hour had come, the little fellow had struck back valiantly. Belgium might even have been compared favourably with other neutral countries who failed to enforce the respect of their frontiers or to take sufficient precautions in good time. She would perhaps not have won the prestige she enjoyed in 1914, but she might have been once more the trusted friend, the loyal ally, who, with Greece, had rendered the greatest service to the common cause.

But success did not follow. King Leopold was faced with failure. It does not matter whether it was his own failure or that of others. Certain failures, at certain times, seem unforgivable.

The constant references to King Albert and to 1914 in every speech or proclamation made by his son during this crisis should not be lightly dismissed. His accusers enlarged upon the cunning way in which he used his father's reputation to conceal his own dark plots, as if he wished to associate the glorious memories of Liège and the Yser to the shameful betrayal of the Belgian campaign.

How did he dare?

Because in all sincerity, he acted as he thought his father would have acted if fate had placed him in the same circumstances.

The more one examines the preamble of the campaign, the more fantastic the legend of betrayal becomes. No one has ever questioned King Leopold's deep devotion to his father, or the sincerity of his religious faith. After warning the guarantor Powers that invasion had taken place and that he intended to defend himself, he sent two short messages, one to President Roosevelt and the other to the Pope. He asked the first, as the "friend of Belgium", to "support with all his moral authority" the efforts which, together with his army and people, he "had now firmly decided to make" in order to preserve the country's independence. He begged the second as the "Head of the Catholic Church, to sustain with his high moral authority the cause for which Belgium was fighting with an indomitable will."

Those who are aware of the relationship binding a Christian to the Head of his Church and more particularly a Roman Catholic to his "Holy Father" should have some difficulty in believing that this message could have been worded in this way if it had concealed a treacherous intention. There are certain limits which even the most ruthless duplicity cannot infringe. Such a display of sacriligeous cynicism would appear as sheer waste of energy in the most confirmed criminal. It could only be the result of mental disorder in a man whose record stood stainless in the light of modern publicity.

"As did his father in 1914," he did not hesitate when the signal was given. According to his constitutional duty, he assumed at once the direction of the country's defence which he had patiently prepared during the last years. He had received the tragic news, during the previous night, having been warned by the Belgian military attaché in Berlin. He did not waste a moment. The Powers notified, his protest sent to his two great moral supporters, his proclamation issued to his people, he left the Palace for his Headquarters, after a last talk with his Prime Minister and two members of his Government. No discussion was needed, a common decision having been reached between them long before.

King Albert was given more time, for German methods have improved since 1914. When he appeared before the Parliament, there was still a faint hope that Germany would not dare to put her threat into execution. The *Blitz* took the place of the ultimatum. King Leopold felt that he had no time to spare when his capital was being bombarded, and his country invaded by the most powerful army in the world. Every Belgian knew that "the King is the Commander-in-Chief of the Army" in wartime and that, according to a tradition established by the dynasty, this right had become a sacred duty. In order to fulfil this duty, King Leopold had to join the Army without further delay.

After May 28th, some writers based their belief in his treason on the following circumstances: (*a*) He had insisted "against the advice of his Cabinet" on assuming the command of his troops. (*b*) He had left the capital without "appearing before Parliament". (*c*) In his proclamation of May 10th, he had not abused the Hun with the same violence as M. Reynaud. (*d*) He did not duplicate his proclamation by a broadcast speech.

These points were solemnly discussed during the weeks which followed the tragedy. They have lost a great deal of their interest to-day. Had the King acted differently, he would have been found equally guilty (*a*) for betraying his duty as Commander-in-Chief, under the Constitution, (*b*) for speechifying instead of acting, (*c*) for indulging in hysterical denunciation unworthy of the position he occupied, (*d*) for wasting his own time and that of his people when more urgent work was at hand.

Chapter VI

THE BELGIAN CAMPAIGN

"ALL ALONG the Albert Canal," writes R. Goffin,[1] "the Belgian soldiers, unaware of the impending catastrophe, were fast asleep. The sentries looked up at the pure May sky. The water in the canal shimmered like quicksilver.

"At twenty past twelve, telephones broke the silence. The officers, half-asleep, picked up the receiver.

"What's the matter? Can't you leave us alone?

"Call your men. On the alert.

"The men grumbled: 'Another stupid rehearsal.'— 'Oh, let's get it over.'

"The 7th Division occupied positions along the Meuse, north of Liège.

"The soldiers soon began to laugh in the clear night: 'I want my five days' leave.'—'I wish they'd chuck these night drills.'

"At 1.30 the telephones began to whisper a certain name to every post, in towns, villages, at the crossroads, near the bridges, in the forts: 'René.'

"The colonels summoned their majors: 'You've heard: "René." It's true this time.'

"In barracks and billets, the non-commissioned officers called their men: 'René . . . René.'

"In a few minutes the sound of that name had

---

[1] *Le Roi des Belges a-t-il trahi?*

passed from the lips of the Chief of Staff to those of the last soldiers: 'René . . . René.'

"Everything proceeded from that name. It filled the echoes. This time, it was war. Every one went to his post, in silence. . . . Suddenly, the fort of Eben-Emael fired six times so that every man should know that the country had been attacked. . . ."

1. *The Flying Bridge*

Speaking of the Albert Canal and of Eben-Emael reminds me of a bridge which played, at one time, an important part in the Leopoldian legend. This bridge was commanded by a strong fort which had been built for the purpose of preventing the crossing of the Meuse south of Maastricht, and of the Albert Canal in the same sector. In 1914, the Germans had been able to cross the river in this region, North of Visé, owing to the fact that the ring of the Liège forts had not been completed according to the plans of General Brialmont; and the Belgians had built Eben-Emael to guard against a similar move.[1]

So much paper has been wasted on this question that it is not without some hesitation that I venture to give here the explanation which has finally been accepted in Belgian military circles and by most British military experts. The story of a treachery, although plausible, was untrue; the following story, less easy to believe, happens to be true. On May 10th, at dawn, a number of German gliders carrying from 10 to 15 men came over the frontier. Some of them flew towards Eben-Emael, others, later in the morning, towards the three principal bridges crossing the Albert Canal west of

[1] See Sketch I.

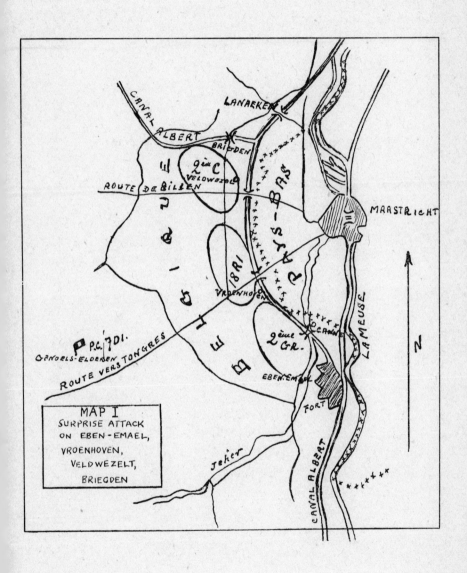

MAP I

SURPRISE ATTACK
ON EBEN-EMAEL,
VROENHOVEN,
VELDWEZELT,
BRIEGDEN

Maastricht. The soldiers manning the gliders succeeded in landing close to the fort and in blowing up the cupolas. They were followed by waves of aeroplanes which released heavy bombs and obtained a series of direct hits which completely wrecked the inner works. Finally, a crowd of parachutists succeeded in penetrating the fort and overwhelmed the garrison which only surrendered the next day.

The bridges of Veldwezeldt, Vroenhoven and Briegden were surprised in the same way, the detachments guarding them being attacked from the rear by gliders and parachutists, and the officers in charge killed before they had time to blow them up. As soon as the General of the 7th Division realized that, owing to the capture of the bridges, the whole Belgian position along the Canal might be turned by the enemy, he ordered their immediate destruction. We are told that a first attempt made by a strong detachment failed to reach its objectives, and that a second attempt made under cover of night, succeeded at Veldwezeldt, thanks to the sacrifice of an officer who perished in the undertaking. The second bridge, at Vroenhoven, was only destroyed at great cost two days later by the R.A.F.,[1] when the enemy was already able to use the bridges crossing the Meuse west of Liège.

It is a heroic story showing the reckless audacity of the enemy and the stubborn courage of Belgian sap-

[1] The names of two gallant officers have been mentioned in this respect: Flying Officer Garland, V.C., and Sergeant Gray, V.C., They both lost their lives in this operation.

A Belgian squadron had previously lost in the same operation, 11 aircraft out of 12.

143

pers and British airmen in their efforts to retrieve the situation. One can only regret that it was used by a number of publicists to shift the responsibility of French reverses upon the shoulders of the Belgians.

I spoke of a "flying bridge", as I might have spoken of the "Flying Dutchman", because in the feverish hurry of the moment, most writers seem to have forgotten to consult their atlas. They had some excuse. The Albert Canal had only been completed two years before, and did not figure on most maps. In the sketches published by some papers, it joined the Meuse north of Maastricht. These writers should have remembered, however, that the latter town is in Holland, and not blamed the Belgians for not destroying the "Maastricht bridge" when they chose to place it there.

A distinguished British author, in his eagerness to explain French reverses, pursued that bridge with particular eagerness, but it seemed to elude his search. It appeared, on June 2nd, "in front of Maastricht," wherever that may be, to reappear on June 16th "above" that town, and at another time "probably near Visé". Anyhow, its non-destruction was the cause of all the trouble. We were told that it was due to "folly or treachery", and that kind M. Reynaud had not alluded, on May 22nd, to the "primary and catastrophic error of leaving the Belgian bridge intact on the lower Meuse", in order not to hurt Belgian feelings. In his magnanimity, he had placed on his own generals the blame for events for which the Belgians were mainly responsible, those Belgians who, by not entering into military conversation with the Allies, and by "objecting to the full organization of the

French frontier" had jeopardized the whole campaign. This author who admitted that his information emanated from French sources, was most eloquent in making the "catastrophe" of Sedan-Calais grow out of the local reverse on the Albert Canal. There seems to have been one bridge only in his mind. It is all the more to be regretted that, to the very last, he remained doubtful concerning its exact position.

Had I as much imagination as this distinguished writer, I might suggest that these articles were part of a conspiracy directed against my King and country by M. Reynaud's French and British propagandists. But, lacking imagination, I prefer to think that the legend grew as legends usually grow when the ill-wind of disaster is sweeping over a country, and that this writer, in all good faith and sincerity, played his pre-destined part in stimulating its growth.

A connection was, nevertheless, established by these attacks, between neutrality and neutralism or defeatism. The results achieved by German parachutists behind the front provoked a crop of stories on the devastating activity of a mythical fifth column, and the initial reverse on the Albert Canal was converted into a major defeat, bringing about with it the breakthrough at Sedan and the cleavage between the "Armies of the North" and the main body of French Forces.

2. *From the Albert Canal to Sedan*

Many errors might be avoided if politicians were given some time to collect their information before speaking on important events and if journalists were not compelled to rush into print so fast. People want fresh news, and this news must be delivered at their doorstep with the milk, every morning. Unfortunately, while milk does not suffer from quick delivery, news often does.

Military experts agree to-day that the surprise attack on the Albert Canal was not a "catastrophe", but merely a setback. The fortified canal was the covering line of the Belgian defences in the north and, without undue optimism, it might have been expected to hold up the first onslaught of the enemy for three days, when Allied reinforcements would have strengthened the position. It was certainly regrettable that the Belgians were obliged to abandon it on the second day of the conflict, and, after strong rear-guard action, to retire on their main line extending from Antwerp to Namur and covering Brussels, but this misfortune did not seriously affect the ultimate result of the operations.

"After a battle of thirty-six hours," wrote Major-General Michiels, Chief of Staff of the Belgian Army,[1] "the Germans broke through our line of defence. Armoured units flowed into this breach, threatening our whole position on the Albert Canal from the rear. . . . The French and British troops had neither the time nor the opportunity of co-operating in this action. This intervention was expected to take place *on the third day*, and had as its first objective to take up battle

---

[1] It will be remembered that, according to the legend, the same General Michiels had opposed the King's decision taken on the 27th and "refused to sign the order given to the troops to lay down their arms".

position on the Meuse, south of Namur, and on the line Namur-Louvain."

One conclusion to be drawn from this straight-forward account is that, short of occupying Belgian territory before the aggression, the Allies could not have prevented this reverse. No "pre-arranged plan", no "military conversation", could have countered the novel methods used by the enemy in seizing, on the morning of May 10th, the main bridges crossing the Canal, and in destroying the fort which commanded them.

Another conclusion is that the break-through on the Maastricht-Tongres road was not in any way the cause of the break-through at Sedan. The confusion made between the Veldwezeldt, Vroenhoven and Briegden bridges, mentioned above, and the "undestroyed bridges" mentioned by M. Reynaud in his speech of May 22nd, partly fostered this new legend. The battle of May 10th–12th between the Belgians and Germans was waged in Belgian Limburg, west of the lower Meuse; the battle of Mézières-Sedan was waged, on May 13th–14th, by the French against the Germans on French territory, on the upper Meuse. The first ended in a gradual retreat upon well prepared posi-tions where the Belgian army joined the bulk of the British and the French in the North. The second ended in complete confusion.

This Antwerp-Namur position, known as the K-W line, was 90 miles shorter than the first line held by the Belgians (Antwerp-Albert Canal-Meuse). It had been considerably strengthened during the first months of the war and the Belgian Staff was convinced that, if the Allies sent sufficient reinforcements, it could be held successfully for a long period of time. This hope might have been confirmed, in spite of the superiority which the enemy had obtained in the air, if the break-through at Sedan and the race of the German mechanized divisions to the sea had not compelled the group of Armies in the North to abandon the K-W line two days after reaching it. They were not even given the chance of making a stand.

"The German mechanized troops," wrote G. Waterfield,[1] "advanced rapidly down the Belgian Meuse and Albert Canal, entering French territory in the Sedan region on May 14th and driving a salient into the French defence lines."

The *Blitz* did not follow such devious routes. It cut right through the Ardennes and reached the upper Meuse, three days after the beginning of the invasion. The reason for the defeat at Sedan must not be sought in the North, and the German mechanized units which appeared on the Meuse south of Namur were not the same as those which drove their way through the Albert Canal.[2]

Mr. Liddell Hart, in *Dynamic Defence*, has shown that the French débâcle was caused by the illusions entertained in French military circles concerning the inaccessibility of the Ardennes region: "General Gamelin pushed his whole left wing, including the British, forward into Western Belgium. He left his centre, facing the Ardennes, almost unguarded. In taking this course, he acted on the conventional idea

[1] *What Happened to France.*
[2] See Sketch II.

148

that, as the Ardennes was difficult country, . . . the Germans would not come that way. . . . Whereas twenty French and British divisions had been pushed forward to support a similar number of Belgian divisions on the sixty mile front between Antwerp and Namur, one of the divisions facing the Ardennes was stretched over twenty miles of front!"

The German staff must have been informed of this grave strategic error, and appear to have encouraged it by retarding their main attack on the Armies in Flanders until the enveloping movement of their motorized divisions had been completed (May 21st).

As a result, General Gamelin was compelled to order the Allied Armies to leave the line Antwerp-Namur and to retire towards the Scheldt. This order was only sent on May 15th at night, two days after the débâcle south of Namur, too late to allow the armies in the North to join the main body of the French armies. This is made evident by M. Reynaud's speech, on May 22nd. Owing to "incredible mistakes", the Army under General Corap, holding the upper Meuse, had been thrown into a "state of complete disorganization", and the German motorized divisions allowed to "rush towards the sea . . . threatening the Allied Armies still engaged in Belgium, which were only ordered to retire on May 15th in the evening." On June 15th, Mr. Churchill, in the House of Commons, further explained that the final disaster was due to the defeat at Sedan and to the fact that General Gamelin did not "withdraw the Northern Armies from Belgium" until two days later.

Things have been restored to their proper perspective. It has been shown that the surprise attack, on May 10th, in the region of Maastricht, did not disorganize the British and French forces which had not yet reached the Albert Canal. It inflicted a reverse on certain units of the Belgian Army which retired in good order upon their second line, the K-W. Its twenty-two divisions occupied the Northern sector from Antwerp to Louvain, with the nine divisions of the B.E.F., on their right, and the Ist and IXth French Armies further south. The forts of Liège had not ceased firing.

The fate of the Belgian Army was decided neither on the Albert Canal nor on the Antwerp-Namur line. It was decided on the upper Meuse, south of Namur, and at Abbeville, outside Belgian territory.

3. *Unity of Command*

Every fresh detail added to the legend sprouted from some misinformation or lack of information. After the surrender of the Belgian Army, a great deal was written and much more was said of the King's unwillingness to co-operate with the Allies. He had made it a condition that he should remain sole master of the movements of his troops. M. Daladier had flown to Belgian Headquarters to "pacify the irate monarch" who was described as "sulking in his tent, like another Achilles"; for the same purpose, Sir Roger Keyes, the hero of Zeebrugge, who had been in close touch with King Albert twenty-two years ago, was sent to Belgian Headquarters to see "whether he could manage to do something with the Belgian Sovereign".

Considering the "incredible mistakes" made not

only by French divisional commanders, but by the Generalissimo himself, a certain reluctance on the part of the Belgian Commander-in-Chief to obey blindly French instructions would have been understandable. But the problem did not even arise. It had been settled at a meeting held at Casteau, near Mons, on May 12th. I have never been able to trace the origin of the Achilles myth, neither can I explain why the results of the Casteau conference were scarcely mentioned in the Press at the time. If full publicity had been given to them the rumour of "Leopold's sulks" would have died a natural death, and M. Daladier's journey would have been accepted without arousing suspicion. Once more, lack of information favoured the legend.

According to a French official report, the following were present: the King of the Belgians, General van Overstraeten, M. Daladier, General Georges, General Billotte, General Champon, General Pownall, Chief of Staff of the British Army. The report adds that both the King and General Pownall agreed that General Billotte, in command of the 1st French Army Group, should be entrusted by General Georges (in command of the North East Front) to "insure the co-ordination of the Allied Armies in Belgium and Holland".

Translated into ordinary language, it means that the French summoned this meeting in order to extend to Belgium the arrangement which had already been working for eight months in France. In this war, as in the last, they attached great importance to unity of command. It had, besides, always been taken for granted that the Generalissimo would direct operations in Belgium in the event of an invasion. His instructions would reach the King through General Billotte, and General Billotte would receive his through General Georges. General Champon, who was also present, was at the Head of the French Mission at Belgian Headquarters, and acted therefore as liaison between King Leopold and French Head-quarters. Achilles did not only consent to act under Agamemnon, but under Agamemnon's subordinates.

The Belgian Sovereign was now Commander of the Belgian army and it was in this capacity that he had come to Casteau. His troops were equalled in numbers by the Franco-British forces which had entered Belgium on the morning of the invasion. He could therefore feel no humiliation in being placed on the same footing as the British, and there is no evidence that he even hesitated in accepting this position, in order to avoid delays or misunderstandings in operations requir-ing centralized information and quick decisions. He did not feel that he was asked to subject himself to a discipline. If unity of command had not already existed, he would have advocated its adoption. Here, once more, he could rely on a precedent, remember-ing how his father had accepted the Command offered him by General Foch, in 1918.

The King received his instructions from General Gamelin on the 15th, and abandoned at once the K-W line and his good towns of Antwerp and Brussels. He received them later from General Weygand, as long as General Billotte lived, and, after his death, as long as General Champon could communicate with General Blanchard. These instructions, whether sent by

Gamelin or Weygand, spoke of nothing but resistance without relief, and more fighting without respite. At last, after having exhausted all his reserves and appealed vainly for support, after having warned the Supreme Command repeatedly for several days, finding himself entirely surrounded by the enemy, the King was compelled to capitulate in order to avoid a useless massacre. For this action he was denounced as a traitor and a coward.

4. *Ordered to Retire*

Legends thrive on misinformation or lack of information and, in certain cases, the censorship encourages instead of checking their growth. What has been said of the "prolongation of the Maginot Line" and of "Leopold's sulks", applies equally well to the "K-W Line". Every one thought, in May 1940, that the main line of Belgian defences ran from Liège to Antwerp along the Albert Canal, because this disposition had been consolidated during the years which preceded the war. Consequently, when the Germans succeeded in crossing the canal and destroying the fort of Eben-Emael, this reverse assumed the proportion of a catastrophe. Some British military writers shared the common belief that it was on the Albert Canal that the main effort of the Allied forces was destined to take place, and that the loss of the position, owing to negligence or treachery, had jeopardized the success of the whole campaign. The Belgians who had "appealed for help" had not even been able to hold on long enough in order to give this help any chance of success. It was a story, at best of improvidence and incompetence, at worst of slackness tinged with fifth column defeatism.[1]

What actually happened was very different. As soon as the war broke out, in September '39, the King and his advisers realized the danger of pinning the whole army on positions extending over 125 miles, at a great distance from the French frontier, and which would become particularly vulnerable if the Germans succeeded in breaking Dutch resistance. The arc formed by the Albert Canal and by the Meuse increased still further the danger of a simultaneous attack from the North and from the South, which might isolate the Belgians from the Allied troops coming to support them. It was therefore decided that this first line would be preserved as a covering position, while a shorter line running from Antwerp to Namur and prolonged in a straight line by the Meuse valley from Namur to the French frontier would become the main position of resistance. With no undue optimism, it could be expected that the Allies could reach this position before

---

[1] *Cf.* M. W. Fodor's *The Revolution is On*: "The *complete débâcle of the Belgian Army within the first hours* of the totalitarian war must have been known to the British and French general staffs . . . Why did the two general staffs send their armies into positions which *already on May 12th* were known to be traps?"

The author tells us that the advance line on the Belgian frontier, in the Ardennes, was expected to hold the enemy for "five days" and that the "fortress town of Louvain" was destroyed by German bombers on May 12th, before the British reached it. Before the invasion King Leopold had been "tipped off by German emissaries and by a German lady friend".

This book appeared in April 1941.

the third day of the struggle. This decision implied cruel sacrifices, the abandonment of half of the Belgian territory to the invader and the almost certain destruction of the country's principal towns, including Brussels, Antwerp, Louvain, Malines and Namur, but it was taken without hesitation as the best means of preserving the country's independence in close co-operation with the French and the British.

While Belgium was accused of pursuing a sub-servient policy, during the first eight months of the struggle, her soldiers and engineers were working feverishly on the construction of this "iron wall". By the spring of 1940, the whole line was fully organized with a multitude of works, scattered on a great depth, anti-tank obstacles, underground telephone systems, and a new network of roads. The K-W, so called be-cause it began at Koningshoyt, near Antwerp, and ended at Wavre, north of Namur, was spoken of with bated breath in Belgium as the surprise kept in store for Hitler if he crossed the frontier. It was not advertised abroad because there seemed no particular reason to give the future enemy this information, and because this new proof of energy might have provided him with a pretext for invasion, before the works could be completed. This explains the misconception which arose as soon as hostilities began, as to the relative strength of the two lines and the part they were destined to play in the country's defence.

The King, who had taken up his Headquarters at Breendonck, was by no means discouraged by the first day's operations. He had noticed with satisfaction the determination shown by his troops in counter-attacking the enemy and delaying his advance. The Allies were now at their side. On May 13th, he issued an Order of the Day in which, after dwelling on the capital importance of the operations pursued during the last three days, he expressed his conviction that "however severe the hardships" imposed upon his soldiers, "they would overcome them valiantly". "Our position improves every hour," he wrote, "our ranks are closing up. During the decisive days of the forthcoming battle, you will stiffen your energy and accept all sacrifices, in order to stop the invader. As on the Yser in 1914, the French and British troops rely upon it. The salvation and the honour of the country command it."

By that time, the K-W line was being manned, the Belgians insuring the defence of the Northern sector (Antwerp-Louvain), the British that of the centre including Louvain, and the First French Army that of the Southern sector up to Namur, where the Belgians once more took charge of the forts and intervals. The "iron wall", as the K-W was called, was held by troops almost equal in numbers, if not in equipment, to those opposed to them. The morale of the Belgians was not shaken by their initial reverse, and the men felt that they were at last in a position to counter German methods of attack which were by now well-known to them.

Just at the time when hope was reviving, on May 14th, two pieces of bad news reached Belgian Headquarters. In the North, the Dutch Army had been compelled to surrender after four days' fighting, and the French Seventh Army was retiring in disorder from Dutch Brabant, uncovering the posi-

tion of Antwerp. In the South, the French line had been forced back in the region of Sedan and pierced from south of Namur to Mézières. German mechanized forces had pushed towards St. Quentin. Unless their progress were checked the Armies of the North might, at any time, be threatened with encirclement and compelled to leave the "iron wall".

The order to retire was, in fact, sent on the 15th in the evening, by General Gamelin. Its effect on the morale of the Allied armies holding the K-W line has not always been appreciated. Soldiers are not so easily deceived as civilians by the vague optimism of official communiqués. They realize that something has gone wrong if they are compelled to abandon well prepared positions which have not yet been heavily attacked by the enemy.

The blow was specially hard to bear for the Belgians who had worked for months on strengthening this line which protected the heart of their country. When the King had agreed to follow the Generalissimo's instructions three days before, at Casteau, he could scarcely have imagined that the first order he would receive would be to allow the enemy to proceed further into Belgium, transformed once more into a battlefield and exposed to all the horrors and ravages of mechanized warfare.

His Chief of Staff, in his memorandum written at his Headquarters of Saint André, on June 1st, records the brutal facts without a word of comment: "On May 15th, the French abandon the defences of the region of Namur. On May 16th, the British retire on Brussels, the French retire between the Sambre and the

Meuse, the Seventh French Army retires on Antwerp from Holland. . . . Exposed by these events, the Belgian Army falls back, step by step, towards Ghent, fighting successful rearguard actions upon the Nèthe, the Rupel, the Willebroeck Canal, the Scheldt and the Dendre, drawn every day further towards the West, owing to the necessity of maintaining contact with the forces operating on its right and left. In spite of the destruction of roads and bridges, the pressure of the enemy becomes stronger every day. From May 18th to May 20th, having taken their appointed positions on the Scheldt and in front of Ghent, the Belgians withstood all attacks while, upon the Oise, the operations were taking place which were to lead to the division of the Allied Armies into two separate groups."

The last sentence is characteristic. It shows the feeling of powerlessness which must have pervaded British and Belgians, as they realized that they were not masters of their own destinies, and that their fate was being decided elsewhere. It is hard enough for a soldier to suffer for his own mistakes, it is much harder to suffer and to see his country suffer for the mistakes of others.

"All troops who cannot advance," proclaimed General Gamelin, at this juncture, "must die at their posts rather than abandon the portion of national soil entrusted to them." But many French officers were by now unable to discover the part they had to play in the confusion which prevailed.

This Order of the Day stands in strange contrast with the communiqués sent from Paris and reproduced in the British Press. One of them (16th, in the

morning) told us that "the battle, in the region of Namur-Sedan, had taken the character of a war of movement", and that "in the interest of military operations it was impossible to publish, at present, precise information". The next day, the war of movement had become a "regular mêlée".

It is important to keep constantly in mind this contrast between the tragic reality which faced the armies in the field, and the befogging form in which it was represented to the people at home, in order to understand the reaction which followed M. Reynaud's speech, like a discharge of electricity.

5. *The Last Days*

While people in London and Paris were talking glibly of the "two Allied fronts" and discussing the possibility of reuniting them, the Belgians and British along the Scheldt and the Terneuzen Canal were really making a last stand, and the latter already contemplated evacuation.[1]

Weygand had replaced Gamelin and M. Reynaud was preparing to dispel before the Senate the illusions which his own propaganda had fostered since the beginning of the campaign. On the 21st, while the Germans reached Abbeville, thus cutting the last link between the Allies, an important conference took place at Ypres during which Weygand explained to King Leopold the plans he had made to cut through the German Panhandle and restore the situation. While he would attack from the South, near Albert, some

[1] From *The Diary of a Staff Officer*, it appears that the B.E.F. was already "organizing" evacuation on May 20th.

159

British and French divisions would attack from the North, near Arras. The Belgians, who defended the Northern sector of the Allied front, were not in a position to take a direct part in the projected offensive, but the King assumed the heavy task of protecting the left flank of the Allies while they were engaged in these operations. In order to release British divisions for the attack the Belgian sector was extended from 31 to 56 miles. By thus stretching dangerously his own front at the time when his troops already suffered from the exhaustion of a painful retreat, the King took an important share in the projected offensive upon which depended the fate of the Northern Armies. It was already obvious that the Belgians could not sustain this effort for long if the enemy chose to launch against them his severest attacks, which he did two days later.[1]

Another conference took place, between the King, Lord Gort and General Billotte. It was immediately after this meeting that General Billotte was killed in a motor accident.

In view of the accusations directed against the Commander-in-Chief of the Belgian Army after the capitulation, it should be pointed out that he took these heavy risks at a time when only one out of the nine

[1] The Laeken memorandum states that, on May 20th, the King had already "advised London of his preoccupations". On the 25th he sent to London "a categorical message" further explaining the eminent peril and "his intentions for the future." This refers no doubt to the letter to King George entrusted to Sir John Dill. On the 19th M. Gutt had already urged M. Reynaud in Paris, to hasten the counter-attack. The same Minister conferred with Lord Halifax, in London, on the critical situation of the Belgian Army, on the 24th.

Belgian provinces had not yet been conquered and for the sole purpose of contributing to the greatest extent possible to the Allies' war effort. He was, however, encouraged by the fine resistance opposed by his troops who, according to a British communiqué, issued the same day, had "largely contributed to the success of the defensive battle" waged on the Scheldt.

Owing to heavy enemy attacks, the B.E.F. was soon compelled to retire from the Scheldt to take new positions upon the Lys, while the Belgians held the southern reaches of the stream and the Lys Canal, with the support of one French division. According to General Michiels's memorandum "all the available units were on the front, the reserves including only units which had been severely shaken by previous fighting".

The German Command, while widening the Panhandle between the two groups of armies and pushing its mechanized divisions along the coast towards Calais, attacked relentlessly first the British and later (from May 24th) the Belgian front.

The 25th is a crucial date. It was the last day on which the Allied counter-offensive from Arras and Albert, postponed from day to day, could possibly take place. On the 24th the Germans had attacked the Belgians heavily at Courtrai and had almost succeeded in driving a wedge between them and the British left flank. The Belgians informed British Headquarters that they would not be able to extend their front in the sector of Menin, as they had hoped to do, and "Lord Gort saw that he had no alternative but to use the two divisions . . . which he had allocated to the southern attack, to stop the gap on his left. He informed General Blanchard that the divisions would not be available for the attack planned, and he feared that, in the circumstances, the French would not attack. Such was indeed the case . . ."[1]

General Weygand's plan never materialized. It seems as if the Generalissimo had given up all hope of realizing it, and the rumour began to spread that he meant to cut his losses—the latter including a million Belgians, British and Frenchmen who were pushed every day closer to the sea and entirely surrounded by a narrowing "ring of iron".

The main German onslaught was now launched against the Belgians, exhausted by eighteen days' fighting and discouraged by a series of costly retreats. The enemy used against them, besides its tanks, a swarm of bombers and fighters which met with practically no opposition, the Belgian aircraft having been completely destroyed and the R.A.F. being kept too busy elsewhere to be able to give any active support.

The Belgians had fought brilliantly on the Scheldt and won the praise of both British and French. They still held on desperately, retrieving the situation at Courtrai with the help of the British, but they were reaching the end of their endurance.

King Leopold realized the danger. He had witnessed a few ominous scenes of confusion, and knew that certain units had given themselves up without waiting for the order of doing so. He had begged Weygand to hasten his counter-attack, he had asked for help against air bombardment. He was only told to hold on. How long?

[1] "Strategicus": *War for World Power*, pp. 271–272.

He knew that, in the leaflets thrown over the Belgian line, the Germans told his troops that "the war was over for them", and that "their leaders would fly away" (*Vos chefs vont s'enfuir par avion*). He realized that, if he left the front, the knowledge of his departure might cause a disaster. In answer to the enemy's challenge, he drew up the following order of the day, issued on May 25th, and which I was not able to publish in this country before July 1st.[1] It explained a good many things which had remained obscure hitherto:

"SOLDIERS,

The great battle which we expected has begun.

It will be hard. We shall wage it with all our power and supreme energy.

It takes place on the same ground upon which we victoriously faced the invader in 1914.

Soldiers,

Belgium expects that you will do honour to her flag.

Officers and Soldiers,

Whatever happens, I shall share your fate.[2]

I ask from everyone fortitude, discipline, and confidence. Our cause is just and pure. Providence will help us.

Long live Belgium!

LEOPOLD

In the Field, May 25th 1940."

This appeal was heard. Not only did the troops pursue their resistance but counter-attacks were de-

[1] *Contemporary Review.*
[2] The Italics are mine. A.

163

livered and several hundred prisoners captured. The communiqué of the next day reflects this stiffening of the resistance: "In spite of the many and hard struggles which have been fought during the last two weeks . . . the forces have maintained their strength and morale."

But, from that moment, the King's fate was sealed. He had given his word.

At that time, as it appeared from his interview with the members of the Belgian Government, the King entertained no illusions concerning the possibility of receiving further Allied support. The "great battle" which had begun the day before was to be the last battle of the campaign. It was waged for vindicating the honour of the Belgian Army and allowing the B.E.F., and some units of the French Army, a short respite which would allow them to reach Dunkirk. Every Belgian soldier who fell in this unequal and desperate struggle fell to save the lives of British and French soldiers. In order to encourage his men to make this supreme sacrifice, the Sovereign gave up everything, even his freedom and his reputation. The struggle was kept up during three full days (24th–28th), and only those who resisted German mass attacks at the time can realize the losses and sufferings involved. These three days saved thousands of men who would never have seen the shores of England again, if the Belgians had not stood between them and the enemy.

Chapter VII

THE SURRENDER

1. *Divided Duty between the Belgian and Allied Armies*

SHAKESPEARE describes better than any other tragic poet the conflict of passions. Some of Racine's greatest works dwell on the clash between passion and duty. Corneille, on the other hand, describes the struggle of man between two conflicting duties. The tragedy of King Leopold is a Cornelian tragedy, but Corneille himself never conceived a more heartrending situation than the one in which the Belgian Sovereign found himself placed from the moment when all hope of reconstituting a common Allied front had disappeared. He had not only to weigh his responsibilities as Head of the State against his responsibilities as Head of the Army, he had also to weigh his responsibilities towards Belgium against his responsibilities towards the Allies.

In this respect some confusion has been caused by a statement made by Mr. Cudahy, the American Ambassador in Brussels, who, in his eagerness to present the Belgian case in the best light possible, has in one or two instances, overstepped the mark.[1]

Mr. Cudahy wrote that, since the mission of

[1] See *Sunday Express*, November 24th and December 1st, 1940.

the Belgian army was only to defend Belgian territory, "to have retreated to France, leaving the homeland at the mercy of the invader, would have been perfidy."

If this opinion implies that the Sovereign's actions during the campaign had been solely inspired by his desire to safeguard material interests, it is contradicted by a series of acknowledged facts.

On May 27th, together with his Staff, he reviewed the situation and examined how far the Belgian Army had fulfilled the mission from the national and from the international, or Allied, points of view.[1] His prompt acceptance of the unity of command, his readiness to comply with the order to retreat from the Antwerp-Namur line, the seven days' stand on the Scheldt and the Lys, and the care taken to do everything possible to help the Allies up to the last moment, are all further evidence that the King did not interpret his mission in a narrow and selfish spirit. He went on fighting for the common cause when most of his country was invaded. He had made preparations to pursue the struggle upon the Yser. He would have followed his father's example in this respect had not further retreat become impossible. But he could no longer leave his last positions without courting disaster, and the road to France was barred by the iron ring which had by then reached Calais. The question which troubled King Albert, in October 1914, when, after the fall of Antwerp, he was urged to send his army to France to recuperate, did not even arise as far as King Leopold was concerned. He was bound in honour to

[1] See p. 24.

follow the instructions given him by the Generalissimo, at Ypres, on the 21st, which were to defend to the last the line of the Lys and to retire eventually on the Yser. The depth of German penetration and the difficulty of moving hard pressed troops in such a congested area made this retirement impracticable, on the 27th.

Whether we consider the decision to surrender, taken on May 27th, from the Belgian or from the Allied point of view, it was determined by the same reasons, and these reasons were of a purely military character.

"On the 26th," writes General Michiels, "the front is broken through at Iseghem, Nevele, Rondele, Belgerhoek. *We have lost contact with the British west of Menin.*

"On May 27th, the last reserves, scarcely three regiments, are engaged, but the gap between us and the British is broadened. . . . Our troops only give way slowly, inflicting heavy losses upon the enemy. But important gaps occur about noon, towards Meldeghem, Ursel and between Thielt and Roulers. Enemy infiltrations penetrate as far as the headquarters in these sectors. *In the region of Thielt, five miles are undefended,* the road to Bruges is open.

"Losses are heavy, no room can be found for the wounded in our overcrowded hospitals. Our artillery lacks munitions.

"The ring of fire tightens around us. Thousands of refugees, mixed with the local population, fly through a narrow strip of territory exposed in its entirety to shell fire and aerial bombardment. Our last means of resistance is broken under the weight of a crushing superiority; we can no longer expect any support, or any other solution but total destruction. The next day could not have brought about any change since further retirement had become impossible. . . . The troops were completely exhausted and the enemy had absolute mastery in the air. Further fighting would immediately have caused the dislocation of the last units which still possessed some cohesion, and the loss of thousands of lives."

The Laeken memorandum declares that, after 11 a.m., "a large breach appeared in the centre of the Belgian front." It was, in fact, almost cut in two, which further explains the impossibility of retiring on the Yser.

This account tallies with the King's letter to the Pope and President Roosevelt, and with the reports given by the officers and men who, after taking part in the last battle, succeeded in reaching England.

There is, however, one question which needs answering. Since resistance could not be prolonged and the road to France was barred, would it not have been possible for the Belgians to do what the British did with thousands of Frenchmen, leave the Continent for England, and add a strong Belgian contingent to the international forces organized in this country? In other words, could they not have reached the coast and taken to the ships?

From the evidence at hand, preparations to evacuate the B.E.F. had begun as early as May 20th. We have definite information that destructions had already been ordered on the 26th.[1] Dunkirk, with Gravelines and Bourbourg, had been assigned as bases to the Belgians by the High Command, but the accommodation of Dunkirk was far too restricted to allow the evacuation of an extra half million men, and they had been told, on the 25th, that it would no longer be available. Even if they had been able to reach their own ports of Nieuport, Ostend and Zeebrugge, there were no ships available. That door was also closed. The Belgian Army was literally trapped.

What was the sacrifice required from King Leopold by his accusers? The wholesale massacre of his army and of the two million civilians crammed into West Flanders? And what would have been the supposed result of this sacrifice? Perhaps a short delay in the German advance allowing the British and French more time to embark at Dunkirk. Much more likely a rout jeopardizing the evacuation and converting a more or less orderly operation into a wild scramble.

In *Through the Dark Night*, J. L. Hodson, speaking of the surrender of May 28th, suggests the following comparison: "It is as though three men, Belgian on the left, British in the centre and French on the right,

[1] See *Blackwood's Magazine* (November, 1940): "On May 26th, the Colonel called the Company Commanders and said that it had "been decided to extricate the B.E.F. from France by hook or by crook. By this was implied the officers, N.C.O.s and men with such equipment as they could carry on their backs, but nothing else." See also "How the Coldstreams fought in May" (*The Times*, November 23rd): "On the night of the 26th, the Commanding Officer attended a conference at which the withdrawal of the B.E.F. was announced, the principle being that troops were to be saved at the expense of equipment."

169

were opposing a foe which outnumbered them. The struggle is terrific. Suddenly the man on the left throws himself on the ground, leaving the centre man —the B.E.F.—to bear the double burden, and to bear it with practically no warning."

A very adequate description of the events as represented by M. Reynaud's indictment. This is what people imagined to have happened. What actually happened was very different: It is as though three men were defending the gate of a fortified town in which they might find a safe refuge. The two closest to the gate have been repeatedly warned by the one in the rear, who was more severely pressed than they were, that he could not hold out much longer. He realized that the gate was narrow enough for two and far too narrow for three. After a final effort, lasting three days, and after making all preparations to facilitate his companions' escape, this man finally laid down his arms. His enemies took everything from him—his land, his food, his freedom. He comforted himself thinking that he had not lost his honour. He was wrong, for his friends at once turned against him and reviled him as a traitor.

It has been definitely proved that the surrender of the Belgian Army did not cause the retreat upon Dunkirk which had become inevitable from the moment General Weygand's counter-attack did not materialize.

It is now becoming more and more evident that the Belgian Staff were right when they stated, on May 27th, that the sending of a *parlementaire* to the German lines "would give the Allies a respite during the night of May 27th–28th, and a few hours the next morning, a respite which could only be obtained by pursuing the fight at the cost of a catastrophic dislocation of the Army," that is to say, at the risk of a rout and its disastrous consequences. If, in one way, the surrender of the Belgian Army may have hastened the advance of the enemy towards Dunkirk (which is by no means evident), in another way, it certainly "simplified the problem of the evacuation" and contributed to "rob the Germans from winning the super-Sedan victory" which they hoped to achieve.[1]

In weighing carefully the pros and cons of the fateful decision he was about to take, King Leopold considered that the losses involved by a policy of no-surrender would be so heavy that they would not compensate the faint chance that such sacrifices might ultimately be of the slightest help to the Allies. He was guided by a principle which King Albert had expressed on many occasions when he had refused to cooperate in certain offensives. In his answer to such proposals to the French, on November 22nd 1914, May 27th 1917, and April 12th 1918, and to the British, in December 1914, he had always emphasized the fact that he could not, in his position of C.-in-C. of the National Army, sacrifice the lives of his men unless he was convinced that such sacrifice was justified by circumstances. It is in this light that we should interpret King Leopold's words in the closing sentence of his letter of May 28th, to the Pope and to President Roosevelt: "No one has the right to sacrifice human lives uselessly."

The King was "cornered into surrender" because:

[1] See Liddell Hart: *The Current of War.*

(1) He would have failed in his duty in abandoning the line of the Lys.

(2) The Belgians were entirely surrounded and isolated from the British on their right.

(3) They had reached the last stage of physical and moral exhaustion, all reserves having been used up.

(4) They could no longer be supplied with food and munitions.

(5) They could not be protected from constant aerial bombardment, and were already disorganized by German attacks.

Beside these reasons which weighed upon the mind of the Commander-in-Chief and of his Staff, there were other reasons which prompted the King to put an end to the martyrdom of his country. He did not see these soldiers as tools of war but as loyal subjects. In order to urge them to a last effort, he had appealed to them as the Head of the country. By prolonging their ordeal, he also prolonged the ordeal and sufferings of several hundred thousand unarmed civilians, including women and children who were looking upon him as upon their supreme guardian and protector.

Between two evils, he chose the lesser of the two, and he was compelled to do so because he wished to cover to the last the movements of his Allies and to protect their left flank. The idea nevertheless prevails in many quarters that he "exposed" it.

2. *Divided Duty between State and Army*

The second choice before King Leopold was more difficult than the first. Although all evidence shows that it was prompted by the noblest and purest intentions, the future alone will reveal whether it was the wisest the Sovereign could have made under the circumstances, in the interest of Belgium and the Belgian people.

This book is concerned with the analysis and criticism of the Leopoldian legend, and the differences which arose between the King and his Ministers, in May 1940, are only indirectly connectèd with this subject. They certainly influenced the campaign waged against the Sovereign by confusing the issue and by suggesting to a vast number of people that his decision to remain in Belgium was dictated by doubtful or suspicious motives. I must therefore deal with this aspect of the question, but I shall do so without entering into superfluous details since it is essentially a Belgian problem.

According to Article 68 of the Constitution, the King is not only the Head of the State, he is also "in command of the National Forces". On the day of his accession, he swears "to observe the Constitution and the laws of the Belgian people, to maintain national independence and the integrity of the national territory" (Article 80). On the other hand, no act of his can take effect unless it is approved (*contresigné*) "by a minister who, by this alone, makes himself responsible for it." Through a custom confirmed by precedents, the Sovereign is supposed to exert a certain influence in all questions concerning the security of the country, and his supreme control of the Army in wartime had not hitherto been seriously questioned.

In assuming command on September 4th 1939, and leaving Brussels for his Headquarters, on May 10th, 1940, King Leopold fulfilled his constitutional duty, as

173

Leopold I and Albert I had done before him, but as
soon as the necessity of the surrendering of the Army
came within the range of possibilities, he was faced
with a series of problems which had never occurred
before. How far could he take such a decision without
previously obtaining the agreement of his Cabinet?
How far could he conciliate the interest of the State
with that of the Army? Should he consider himself
bound to remain with his men to the last, according to
his promise and to the code of military honour, or
should he follow his Government abroad, as other
Sovereigns placed in similar circumstances had done
recently, in order to remain free to pursue the fight?

These are precisely the questions upon which
differences arose between the King and his Ministers.
These differences prompted M. Pierlot to dissociate
himself from King Leopold's action in his speech of
May 28th.

I have already pointed out[1] that in the questions of
neutrality, military preparations and resistance to the
invasion, the Sovereign and the members of his
Government had been in full agreement. During all
these years, they had worked in the closest co-operation. This co-operation was pursued until May 10th
1940, when the King had a last interview with his
Ministers before leaving for his Headquarters. From
that day, the same contact between them could not be
maintained, owing to the strain put on the Commander-in-Chief and on the Government by rapid
and disastrous military developments. During that
time, the Sovereign was surrounded by officers who

[1] See p. 96.

were more inclined to appreciate events from the military than from the legal or political point of view. The link of mutual confidence had been weakened. The nervous strain imposed upon all by the impending catastrophe did the rest.

Neither should we forget that, if the encircling of the Northern Armies had placed the King-Commander in a cruel dilemma, it had also placed his Government in a most painful situation. They were supposed to endorse decisions over which they had practically no control and the principle of their ministerial responsibility was seriously engaged. They could not, like the French and British Governments, assume the supreme control of operations directed by military commanders, and were at the same time aware that any disagreement, during the campaign, might have disastrous consequences. The history of the last war and of the recent French campaign shows that a certain amount of friction frequently arises between the Prime Minister and the Generalissimo. The danger caused by such differences is increased tenfold if the Generalissimo is the Sovereign himself. In peacetime, the latter does not make a public speech without taking the advice of his Minister who makes himself responsible before the Parliament and the people for everything he says. In wartime, under the Belgian Constitution, the Sovereign may take the gravest decisions, involving the future of the country, and his responsible Minister, if he wishes to interfere, is placed at a considerable disadvantage when his opinions do not agree with those of senior officers.

What happened at the Headquarters of St. André,

on the 20th and 21st, and during the last fateful interview at Wynendael, on the 25th, will only be accurately known when those who took part in them will
choose to speak.[1] Meanwhile, the following account,
given by the *Sept Jours*, a weekly paper published in
Lyons (December 16th 1940) may give some idea,
however incomplete, of these dramatic events.

The first meeting had been "very cordial", but the
conversation dwelt only on generalities. The "possibility of an armistice" was mentioned. The next day,
the Ministers were more insistent: "All agree that a
catastrophe is imminent. But what is the solution?
Pierlot has made his choice: The game is lost in Belgium. The King, as Head of the State, must leave the
Army and go to London and Paris. War must be pursued outside Belgium.

"I am the Chief of the Army," answers the King.
"I shall not leave my men, even if I am made a
prisoner."

"Pierlot insists . . .: The King is the Head of the
State. The war may last a long time. The Ministers
are in France. Must they be condemned to a solitary
exile?' . . . .

"Leopold remains silent. His resolution does not
waver. He has reached his decision and refuses to
pursue the discussion; they part without reaching a
solution, but no doubt is any longer possible: two

---

[1] The King, the Prime Minister, M. Pierlot, the Minister for
Foreign Affairs, M. Spaak, the Minister of War, General Denis,
and M. Van den Poorten, Minister of the Interior. General
Denis, who had taken a large share in military preparations,
remained in agreement with his colleagues.

opposed opinions confront each other. For three long days, the King and his Ministers do not meet."

On the 25th, at 4.45 a.m., "the four Ministers . . . called upon the Sovereign" at the "huge, sombre castle of Wynendael," surrounded by woods, 14 miles from Bruges.

"The King . . . was resting on a couch. Should they wake him? After a moment's hesitation, Pierlot decided that they should.

"They were ushered into a large smoking-room. The King's face betrayed nothing but the expression of a tired soldier who has just been roused from his first sleep. Twenty miles away, the Belgian front is breaking. . . .

"About 5 p.m. they begin to talk. . . . For the last time, Pierlot explains his plan. He will remain with the King until the last moment. When they judge that everything is lost, they will leave together by air.

"Leopold III shakes his head obstinately. He has made up his mind.

"London," he says, "has been warned; Paris has been warned. There is no dishonour in being beaten as we are beaten. We have a clear conscience. What should I do in London or Paris?

"Public opinion will not understand the King's attitude. The Belgian refugees will be still less inclined to understand it.

"My place is not with the refugees. I must stay with my troops. . . . I cannot abandon six million Belgians and six hundred thousand soldiers for one million refugees and two hundred thousand men of the reserve.

"Pierlot does not acknowledge defeat. He alters his tactics:

"But what power does the King hope to preserve? . . ."

"I intend to look after the prisoners and the economic life of the people . . .

"Nothing can bend his calm, obstinate resolution, ripened in solitude. . . . The case has been heard. . . .

"The Ministers take their leave. They will not return. The separation is final. Each one has chosen the way which he thinks worthy of himself."

However incomplete, this account shows that both parties were equally convinced that they were fulfilling their duty. The soldier wished to remain with his soldiers, to keep his word to them and to save his military honour. The statesmen wished to leave a country where they could no longer fulfil the mission they had undertaken to fulfil. They thought of abstract realities of the State, of the Nation. He thought of concrete realities, of men, women and children. They wished to be where they could still be able to carry on the fight, he wished to be where his soldiers and people were exposed to privations and suffering. The conflict was not moral, but political.

Another point made by the author of this article can be confirmed: M. Pierlot's offer to remain with the Sovereign until the final decision to surrender the Army had been taken. It disposes of the reproach made later to the Belgian Premier, suggesting that he was reluctant to take the risks involved by prolonging his stay in Belgium.

We are now in a better position to understand why M. Pierlot spoke as he did on May 28th. In the light of what he had heard and seen it was difficult for him to doubt that some "negotiations" had actually taken place between the King and the enemy and therefore not to declare at once that his action was unconstitutional and did not bind the Government. Unlike the French Premier, he never hinted at treason and remained convinced that if the Sovereign had committed this fatal error, his motives remained disinterested.

It is significant that at the meeting of the Belgian Parliament held at Limoges, on May 31st, the Government opposed a motion deposing the King and did not even accept an order of the day expressing the wish that his position should be reconsidered after the war. M. Pierlot and his colleagues refused to take any step which would have compromised the monarch at a time when all the facts had not yet been revealed and when the majority of the Belgian people could not be consulted. In the course of this debate and of several consultations they had later with the Belgian Ministers of State who were in France at the time (MM. Hymans and Janson among them), they maintained the same attitude, fully aware of the danger of taking any premature decision which might not be supported by their compatriots in occupied Belgium. The wisdom of this policy was fully confirmed by future events.

The French Premier's speech of May 28th was a political manoeuvre based on a misrepresentation of the facts. The Belgian Premier's speech of the same date was prompted by a sincere belief that the Sovereign had committed a grave error which might jeopardize the future of the country.

3. *Clearing the Air*

Two attacks were made against the King after the surrender, the Franco-British attack based on the legend of military treason and the Belgian attack founded on the unconstitutional character of his action. The King was accused by the Allies of betraying their trust in his conduct of the war, and by a large number of Belgians of betraying his constitutional oath. He had not warned "General Blanchard", and he had entered into negotiations with the enemy against the advice of his responsible ministers.

I was not able to refute the accusations of no warning and to publish extracts of the Laeken memorandum before December 1940[1], and the attitude of the Government towards the Sovereign could not be made clear in this country before the four Belgian Ministers gathered in London in October last. Four precious months were thus lost during which M. Reynaud's indictment flourished almost unchecked.

On June 2nd 1940, a Pastoral Letter issued by the Belgian Primate, Cardinal Van Roey, was read in all the churches of Belgium. In this letter, the Cardinal deplored "the unfortunate misunderstanding" which had occurred, and stated that the King's decision had been taken "in full accord with his Chief of Staff and following his advice":[2]

[1] *Contemporary Review*. Some of the facts mentioned in this article had already been published by M. Cudahy in the *Sunday Express*, late in November.

[2] The legend had spread that General Michiels had refused to sign the order of capitulation and that important units of the army had disobeyed it and pursued the fight.

"He has not performed any political act nor has he concluded any treaty or pact—even of a military nature —with the enemy. He has therefore not violated the Belgian Constitution in any way whatsoever. He acted because, strengthened in his decision by the judgment of three eminent jurists, he was convinced that he had the right to do so in virtue of the power that the Constitution confers on the King in this matter."[1]

This letter, together with other documents, was brought to Switzerland by an envoy who communicated them to Vicomte Berryer, former Counsellor of the Belgian Embassy in Berlin, who had been despatched to Berne to meet him. The envoy of the Sovereign gave further explanations: The King had merely refused to follow his Ministers because, according to him, he could not leave his army. He had not treated with the enemy, but merely laid down his arms. A capitulation is not a treaty. He had wished to save his people. The people had rallied round him. His dignity and his constitutional oath compelled him to remain among them in their misfortune. He denied that he had not warned the Allies and that the surrender had been the cause of a defeat. Such a defeat could no longer be prevented. . . .

The memorandum of the three jurists—M. Devèze, Minister of State, M. Pholien, Senator, and M. Hayoit de Termicourt, Attorney-General of the Supreme Court, was still more explicit. These three experts, who, apart from the positions they occupy, enjoy in Belgium an undisputed reputation, were attached to the army and in a position to appreciate the military as well as the legal situation. Their state-

[1] Appendix XII.

ment, dated June 2nd, must have been prepared immediately before or after the surrender. It only reached this country at the end of June.

The memorandum stated that the King, as Head of the Army, had the right to remain with his soldiers, and to fulfil the promise given in his Order of the Day (May 25th) in order to counter the effect of German propaganda. "By preferring to accomplish his military duty," the statement went on, "to the advantages he might have derived from his departure from the country, the Sovereign gave a magnificent proof of his courage and of his disinterestedness."

On the other hand, the memorandum which must have been communicated to M. Pierlot with the knowledge and approval of the King, recognized that, according to Article 82 of the Constitution, the Executive power devolved entirely upon the Government, now that the Sovereign, a prisoner of war, was temporarily unable to exercise it.

The experts concluded by saying that in the interest of the country and in order to prevent divisions which might easily be exploited by the enemy, "the fatal error which prompted the accusation of breach of Constitution directed against King Leopold should be rectified without delay."

Reading this document, we can only regret that the men who drafted it had not been consulted a few days before. This might have allowed the King to make his position clear from the start and to show the members of the Government that his wish to remain with his men and his people was not irreconcilable with their own attitude.

These communications considerably relieved the tension between the supporters of the King and the supporters of the Government. On the occasion of Belgian Independence Day, on July 21st, M. Pierlot delivered an address in Vichy to a group of Belgian refugees in which he said: "We ardently hope that the wish which will dominate all others in the minds of the Belgians will be that of national union around the King, and that this same sentiment will be felt by all those whose conscience tells them that they have done their duty."

M. Pierlot expressed the wish to broadcast this speech to his compatriots in Belgium, but the French Government of the day did not allow him to do so.

Since then the position of the Belgian Government has been made abundantly clear. "The fate of Belgium," wrote M. Spaak, "is linked up with the destinies of Great Britain. The cause of Great Britain is therefore our cause." In a broadcast message to his compatriots in Belgium, M. Gutt declared that the Government would continue to "struggle for the liberation of Belgium and her King." The country is under enemy occupation, her Sovereign is a prisoner of war.

Belgians are practically unanimous in their belief that the King will not alter the attitude which he has spontaneously adopted since the first day of his captivity. He has refused to govern under the control of the invader, because his power can only be exercised in a free and independent country. It emanates from the Constitution, and the Constitution is non-existent as long as Belgium is occupied by the enemy. This refusal to recognize the accomplished fact is, in itself, a permanent protest and the lesson of this protest is not lost on the people. They rally around the Crown because the Crown has become for them the symbol of resistance.

The divisions which, during the first months of the occupation, prevailed between the henchmen of King Leopold and the henchmen of the Pierlot Government, have lost all bitterness, but they are still used by German propagandists and the few supporters they have been able to enlist, in the forlorn hope of weakening patriotic resistance by exploiting old grievances and suspicions.

4. *The King's last message to his Troops*

On May 27th, at 5 p.m., a Belgian plenipotentiary left Headquarters for the German lines in order to make enquiries regarding the conditions in which hostilities might cease.

He returned five hours later bringing back the German answer: unconditional surrender.

At 11 p.m., after consulting his Staff, the King accepted, and suggested that the "cease fire" should take place at 4 a.m.

Agreement was given to this proposal at 3 a.m.

The protocol signed by General von Reichenau and General Derousseaux has a purely military character: "The Belgian troops will immediately and unconditionally lay down their arms and consider themselves as prisoners of war. An armistice[1] began this morning at

[1] Great play has been made of this word which may mean anything from a straightforward military capitulation, such as this one, to a diplomatic document involving political questions, such as the German Armistice of 1918 and the French Armistice of 1940. It is the nature of the transaction which matters, not the name given to it.

4 a.m. at the request of the Belgian Command. German operations against the French and British troops will not be interrupted.

"Belgian territory, including the ports, will be immediately occupied. No fresh destruction will be carried out on the locks and fortifications of the coast."

An additional protocol stated (1) that the officers would be allowed to keep their arms, and (2) that the castle of Laeken would be placed at the King's disposal, so that he might reside in it with his family and household. Both these concessions had been spontaneously granted without any request being made by the Belgian Commander.

Before leaving his Headquarters and parting from his men, King Leopold drafted a last Order of the Day, which, to my knowledge, has not yet been published in this country, and which is perhaps more valuable than his letter to the Pope, because, for once, he allows himself to relax and reveals some of the feelings which inspired his decision.

Nothing has yet been written of the loyalty which the Belgian soldiers felt towards him and of his affection for them. Not much sentiment has been wasted on the *Blitz*. Events succeeded each other so rapidly during these eighteen days, that those engulfed in them found scarely time for comment. We only know that, following his father's example, the King did not spare himself, and made frequent rounds of inspection. We also know that his officers dreaded his possible departure because, during the last days, his presence at the front was "the only thing which still kept the troops together".

Ties between men thrown into such dangers and suffering grow fast and strong. After a fortnight's separation, certain Belgians who had remained in Brussels during the campaign, found their Sovereign much altered, and no wonder. They had left a statesman, they found a soldier. His men had given their lives for the country, no doubt, but also for him. Had he not appealed to them repeatedly? Had he not sent messages to the defenders of Liège and Namur, asking them to "resist to the last", and had they not resisted? Like King Albert, King Leopold never forgot that he stood in the land as the defender and protector of the common people. He had always been the friend as well as the Commander of his troops. He understood them and they understood him. During the last crisis, weighed down by the responsibilities pressing upon his shoulders, he must have thought that they alone preserved for him something of the devoted loyalty which he had enjoyed during the first years of his reign. He could not desert them, he could not break his promise, he could not tear himself away. They had suffered together. Whatever happened, his duty done, they would go on suffering together.

Queen Elisabeth, his mother, who was in Bruges at the time, is supposed to have said when she heard of the Ministers' visit at Wynendael. "They ask us to leave? How can we leave? Our people are being killed all around us." In 1914, she had only left Antwerp for a few days to bring her children to England. She had gone back to the besieged town, accompanied her husband during the retreat, and shared his simple life, behind the front, at La Panne. The tradition of courage and devotion must go on. The Sovereign should be where his people suffer most. King Leopold inherited his father's strict sense of duty, but he inherited also his mother's sensitiveness. Placed between two duties, he chose the one which coincided with his natural impulse and his deeper instincts:

"Officers, Non-Commissioned Officers and Men: Thrown abruptly into a war of extreme violence, you have fought bravely to defend, inch by inch, the country's territory.

"Exhausted by an uninterrupted struggle against an enemy far superior in numbers and equipment, *we find ourselves cornered into surrender*.

"History will judge that the Army has done its duty. Our honour is safe.

"These fierce battles pursued through sleepless nights cannot have been fought in vain. I order you not to despair and to bear yourselves with dignity.

"Let your attitude and discipline show that you are worthy of a stranger's esteem.

"I remain with you in the misfortune which falls upon us, and I wish to watch over your lives and over those of your families.

"To-morrow, we shall begin to work with the firm resolution of raising the country from her ruins.

LEOPOLD."

How much of this hope is left to him now? He may have been able to soften to a certain degree the hardships of the Belgian prisoners and to hasten their repatriation. He may perhaps exert a certain influence in attenuating the privations and sufferings endured by his people owing to the shortage of food. Apart from that, he can do nothing.

There is one way, however, in which he can help and in which he has already helped his people. His sole presence, even if it brings neither bread nor release, is a comfort to them. He cannot speak to them, he cannot even walk among them, but they know that he is there, in the same prison, sharing their miserable life. Materially he has become powerless, morally he remains powerful.

He has lost everything but, like his father, he has preserved his honour and dignity, this honour and dignity which he urged his soldiers to keep unblemished before the enemy. Let us pray that he will also maintain his hope in the future judgment of the world and in the honesty and fairmindedness of his former friends who have already recognized, or will soon recognize, that their good faith has been waylaid, and that the traitor of the Leopoldian legend is not unworthy to be the son of one of the greatest heroes of modern history.

Side by side with the King's last message to his army should be placed General Weygand's last message to the King.

The Generalissimo had been duly informed through General Champon of the time appointed for the cease fire. The Chief of the French Mission which was in La Panne was instructed to communicate to the Belgian Commander the following telegram: "The French and British Governments agree that their

188

armies should save the honour of the flag in dis-
sociating themselves (*en se désolidarisant*) from the
Belgian Army."

The latter and its Chief had become untouchable.

This blame was inflicted on the Belgian Commander
for having discharged the instructions given him at
Ypres, on the 21st. He had not only defended the
line of the Lys "to the last", but he had also provided
for the defence of the Yser. The orderly retreat of the
Belgians on this line having become impracticable,
the 60th French Division which had been co-operating
with them east of Bruges, was conveyed, behind the
Belgian lines, towards the Yser, on the 27th. The
bridges and locks of the stream had been destroyed two
days before and the flood was rising. At the same
time, two thousand trucks had been placed on the
railway line from Roulers to Ypres across the gap
which separated the British from the Belgians. These
arrangements had been made with the co-operation
of General Champon in order to place fresh obstacles
in the way of the invader, after the surrender.

Meanwhile, the Generalissimo had failed to deliver
his promised counter-attack, and cut his losses.

Chapter VIII

LAEKEN

1. *The Führer's "Present"*

THE SURRENDER of the Belgian Army was unconditional. King Leopold, as a prisoner, had no other choice but to reside where it was his conqueror's wish that he should reside, in the Royal Castle of Laeken. He would have preferred a simpler and more cheerful abode, such as the country house of Stuyvenberg, where he had spent such happy years with his family before his father's death. He was given no choice. Laeken was the "present" which, according to the cartoonists of June 1940, had been conferred upon him by the Führer as a reward for his "betrayal".

Since May '40, he has lead a secluded life in that solemn building overshadowed with old beeches, and in the old-fashioned park which surrounds it. He can wander through these dark avenues, along the damp lawns bordering a lake, dotted with white swans, and, occasionally, play a game of golf on that course on which he used to practice regularly in happier days. He is allowed to see a few friends, but his visitors are met by German sentries at the gate. He cannot leave the grounds without obtaining permission from his gaolers and is naturally reluctant to apply for it. His prison is not merely military and political, it is a place of confinement from which he could only be released on certain conditions which he refuses to accept.

Even ordinary criminals are given some time, every

190

day, to walk round their prison courtyards. The park at Laeken is no doubt less oppressive, but it is not less jealously guarded.

King Albert who was supposed to be pro-French had sent his children to England in 1914; King Leopold who is supposed to be "anti-French", sent them to France in 1940. Let those who still believe in premeditated treason explain this if they can. The children came back to Belgium after the Armistice and their visits are now the Sovereign's main source of comfort.

"This hour in the afternoon," writes an anonymous contributor to the *Sept Jours*,[1] "when Queen Elisabeth and her grandchildren pay a visit to the Royal prisoner, is one of the rare relaxations which the most abused Sovereign in history allows himself since the cruel spring when his country was crucified. . . . For the last six months, he has been completely isolated from a people who, knowing him better than we do, share his preoccupations and anxieties."

There have been reports that he paid a short visit to Ciergnon, in the Ardennes, where his children spent part of the summer. There have been confirmed reports that he went to Germany, in the late autumn, to "confer with Hitler". Believers in the legend in this country and in America eagerly hailed the news, at the time, as a fresh proof that their suspicions had been well founded. Others related a dramatic interview during which the Sovereign proudly refused an offer of the Crown of a puppet state including Belgium, Holland and Luxemburg.

[1] December 14th, 1940.

191

What seems far more likely to be true is that, in the autumn 1940, King Leopold undertook a journey to Berchtesgarden in order to obtain from the conqueror an improvement in the situation of the prisoners and some attenuation of the food situation which was becoming more and more critical. The purpose of such a journey would agree with the last message of the King to his troops, in which he promised to watch over them and their families and to do everything in his power to help them.[1] It also would agree with the answer he is supposed to have given to his Ministers at Wynendael, when he said that he intended to look after the prisoners and the "economic life" of the people.

This visit must have been one of the most cruel trials the King has experienced in this year of trials, for no amount of sympathy and affection for his people could obliterate his pride, and that pride must have been sorely strained when he climbed the long flight of steps leading to the villa where the Führer was waiting for him. We are told that several invitations had been declined before the last one was accepted. We are also told that the interview was extremely formal, each protagonist making set speeches without entering into conversation, or even what would amount to an exchange of views. The Führer delivered his oration in German and the King said what he had to say in French. The atmosphere remained frigid throughout. It was only when all was over, on the way back, that Leopold III allowed himself to relax, and expressed the pleasure he felt in driving in a car—a pleasure which

[1] p.187.

he had not enjoyed for months. One thing is certain: this visit altered nothing in the political status of the country or in the King's personal position. He remains, so far as he is concerned, a prisoner exerting no power and determined to take no part whatsoever in the administration of the country.

2. *"The King does not reign"*

Whether or not, on May 25th, the Sovereign fully realized the consequences of his decision to remain in Belgium, any doubts which he may have had on the subject were quickly dispelled, as appears from the memorandum drafted, as early as June 2nd, by three Belgian jurists attached to the Army.

MM. Devèze, Pholien and Hayoit de Termicourt, while fully justifying the King's action, pointed out that, as a prisoner of war, he was temporarily unable to reign, according to Article 82 of the Constitution. If we keep in mind the early date of this memorandum, we must assume that the Sovereign was aware of the fact when he surrendered his army and that this provision of the National Charter solved the cruel dilemma which had confronted him a few days before.

Since he was deprived of all authority from the moment he fell into the hands of the enemy, he felt sure, at last, that his decision could not affect the political status of the country and that he would not be placed in a false position. By giving up his power as Commander of the Army, he did not resume his power as Head of the State; he gave up every kind of public responsibility. By entering his prison he entered a strictly private life, and would maintain this privacy as long as Belgium remained occupied.

"For the time being, the King does not reign," has become his motto. He has never departed from this attitude and the Belgians who denounced him at the time of the surrender have been the first to recognize that he has done nothing since to confirm their hasty judgment.

The Sovereign may have interceded with the German authorities on behalf of his subjects and generously subscribed to relief funds, such as the *Secours d'Hiver*, but he did this as an individual, in his private capacity. His scruple in this matter goes so far that when he meets any public man, such as his former Minister, M. Delfosse, or the Burgomaster of Brussels, M. Van de Meulebroeck, the successor of Burgomaster Max, and any of the city's aldermen, he refuses to discuss with them any question in which his own opinion might influence their actions. They are received as private friends.

Those who express the regret that the King should no longer exercise his authority or even use his personal influence upon his own subjects meet with the same invariable answer: "The King is no longer the Head of the State. He is a military prisoner unable to exercise any power. As long as this situation exists he will in no way whatsoever interfere in public affairs." The same refusal is opposed to all would-be advisers, whether Belgians or Germans.

We have heard a good deal about "Leopold's stubbornness". If it is to be stubborn to preserve a line of conduct which conforms with one's sense of duty and honour, whether as a neutral, as Chief of the Army or as prisoner of war, the reproach is deserved. The King may be slow to make up his mind, but when his mind is made up, like his father, he is unwilling to alter it. This same strength of character which made him so many enemies, may still bring him many more friends.

3. *Entourage*

The only men with whom the prisoner is in constant and intimate intercourse are those who share his prison life, his collaborators, his secretaries and the members of his household. We know besides that he is in contact with experienced men whose honour and patriotism are above suspicion and whose reputation has been established in the country for many years. Such are, for instance, M. Wodon, who was King Albert's *Chef de Cabinet* and General Tilkens, former Governor of the Congo.

It is necessary to enter into these details, because the name of the King, since the earlier days of his captivity, has been associated with those of certain politicians who are now backing up the New Order with the support of the German authorities. The Socialist leader de Man is one of them, Degrelle, the head of the depleted Rexist Party, is another. Since the Sovereign cannot be compromised, owing to his perfectly correct and consistent attitude, attempts have been made to compromise him through his "close relations" with disloyal subjects. If an objection is made that these rumours rest on no foundations, it is answered that, as King Leopold and Queen Elisabeth had been connected with these persons in the past, "it is not unlikely" that they should continue this connection at present.

I happened to be in Brussels during the partial election of April 1937, which marked the turning point in Degrelle's career. His defeat by M. van Zeeland was a foregone conclusion, but it would never have been so decisive if his methods had not been exposed by King Leopold and Cardinal Van Roey. The Rexist leader had boasted publicly that he enjoyed the support of the Belgian Primate and that the Sovereign shared his opinions. Two categorical denials appeared in the Press on the eve of the poll. So much for the "close friendship" between the King and the man whose hysterical enthusiasm for the New Order has become an embarrassment to the Nazis themselves.

M. de Man is a very different person. Both learned and intelligent, he succeeded in building up for himself a considerable reputation as an economist. He was once considered as the greatest hope of the Socialist Party, the predestined successor to M. Vandervelde. His "plan" of economic and social reconstruction was adopted by the Socialist Congress. He was among the younger men whose collaboration the King enlisted when he asked M. van Zeeland to form his first Cabinet. Later, he was in charge of the department of Public Health, and Queen Elisabeth, who has throughout her life been keenly interested in nursing and child welfare, was frequently seen with him when they inspected hospitals and welfare centres. To-day M. de Man, whose ambition is even greater than his intelligence, is doing his best, under Nazi protection, to disintegrate the Socialist Party, and to use his influence with the Left in the same way as Degrelle is using his with the Right. It matters very little to the Nazis whether the two leaders will ever be able to co-operate in the future. They are out to destroy Belgian public life, not to consolidate it.

In a recent book, M. Jules Romains, relating a visit paid to him by M. de Man, in December 1938, speaks of him as the "King's man," engaged in secret negociations of the utmost importance, of which the Belgian Government was not kept informed. I am in a position to state that this somewhat naïve story is merely a product of the French poet's imagination. Both the King and M. Spaak were aware of M. de Man's self-appointed mission, but never gave him the right to speak in their names.

As late as March 26th, 1941, a contributor to a London evening paper prefaced an otherwise fairly accurate account of King Leopold's present attitude with the following words: "Leopold, King of the Belgians, dreamed of being dictator-King of a semi-Fascist State. He never wanted to be dragged into war. While his democratic people dashed one hope, the Germans destroyed the other. His pro-Axis inclinations—and especially his pre-war liking for Mussolini's Italy—made him mistrusted by the other Western Democracies."

The reader who has had the patience to read the chapter in which I dealt with Belgian neutrality is well aware that the King favoured the change of policy in 1936, not because he wished to please Hitler and dreamt of dictatorship but, on the contrary, because he refused to try and force the hand of his Parliament and public opinion. It was the only way left to him to obtain, by constitutional means, the men and credits necessary for the defence of the country, and of conciliating his duty as leader of the Army with his duty as Head of a constitutional monarchy.

Neither is it possible to contend that the emergency powers given to his Government, under M. van Zeeland's leadership, can be even remotely connected with dictatorial aspirations.

The Government was given "special powers" to deal with financial difficulties in King Leopold's reign, as in King Albert's reign, but these were granted freely by Parliament for a limited period of time and for a special purpose. Far more extensive powers were wielded by the Heads of other democratic states in Europe and America, during the "twenty years' crisis."

There is not a shadow of evidence that the Sovereign entertained dictatorial ambitions. The very fact that he enlisted the services of well-known legal experts to justify his decision of May 28th is a further proof of the importance he has always attached and still attaches to the respect of the Constitution. He has not given his oath lightly and he is not the man to forget it.

The suspicion of "pro-Axis inclinations" does not rest so much on this last action, as on the attitude observed by the Sovereign during the period when he governed the country with the support of a majority including Socialists and Christian Democrats, and when Belgium agreed to apply sanctions against Italy.

But, we are told, his sister had married the Prince of Piedmont and he remained on excellent terms with her! Does it not show that he was pro-Mussolini? All that has been said and written concerning the restraining influence exerted by the Vatican and the House of Savoy on the Italian Dictator has been forgotten since the latter dragged his unfortunate country into the struggle. Neither do we remember to-day the policy pursued for months by Mr. Chamberlain in the hope of conciliating the Duce and of appeasing the Führer. Was Mr. Chamberlain a pro-fascist? And, if not, why should the King of the Belgians be denounced to-day for holding certain opinions in 1936 which led both M. Daladier (no doubt another pro-fascist) and the British Premier as far as Munich in 1938? To add that the fate of democracy does not depend alone on purely democratic countries to-day and that some of our most valuable Allies in the Near East can scarcely be called "democratic" might be beside the point. But, as long as the modern world remains what it is, it is perfectly relevant to observe that a constitutional Monarch may quite well entertain, in peace-time, good relations with the unconstitutional Government of a foreign country without wishing to destroy the guarantees and liberties enjoyed by his own people.

The fact is that the Leopoldian legend is in full retreat, but does not yet acknowledge defeat. Beaten on the question of military treason, it took refuge behind the black battalions of the Fifth Column. Unable to use these shaky reinforcements, it sought protection behind a suspicious neutrality. Now that this last retrenchment is threatened, the legend pursues its desultory attacks in a guerilla warfare in which the rough is mingled with the smooth, and cautious insinuations watered down with sentimental sympathy.

This will not do. The King of the Belgians does not appeal for pity, but for justice. He does not wish to be forgiven crimes which he has not committed. He wishes only that the truth should be established and the facts recognized. If, after these facts have been made clear, the world persists in condemning him, he will accept the world's judgment without bitterness but with the full consciousness that he has not departed from the high standard of morality which he set for himself at the beginning of his tragic career. He would not be the first nor the last man to be the victim of the vagaries of popularity.

4. *"Without a trace of bitterness"*

M. Cudahy was received by King Leopold, at Laeken, two days after the surrender, on May 30th:

"Two days later, I saw the King. Heavy booted German sentries with ill-fitting green-grey uniforms and steel mushroom helmets presented arms, and inside the great doors, a German officer awaited me.

"For the King was a prisoner in his own palace. . . . His captors had brought him back to Laeken.

"He could not conceal his emotion at our meeting. Never had I seen upon a human countenance a more poignant portrayal of grief, as if the ghastly spectacle of the past twenty days had scarred his soul for ever.

"Yet there was about his demeanour no hint of weakness. His eyes held the same unwavering honesty,

200

and unchanged was his erect military bearing, which would always distinguish him as a soldier.

"At length and in full detail he spoke about the débâcle which had brought disaster upon his country. Without a trace of bitterness he mentioned his hostile critics and their condemnation as if, with the wages of war, calumny was to be expected."

It is, no doubt, to be regretted that M. Cudahy was not, or could not be, more explicit, but the tone of his articles confirms their conclusion. The prisoner at Laeken based his defence primarily on military considerations. He had loyally fulfilled the task which had been given to him, and only surrendered when all means of co-operating with the Allies had been exhausted. He insisted that, during the last five days, he had repeatedly given them due warning of the desperate position in which his troops were placed, and that capitulation could not be avoided unless some measure of support reached them in time. He dwelt on the fact that the French units within the Belgian lines had all left for France before the 27th, with the sole exception of the 60th Division, which was conveyed to the Yser on that day, and that the floodgates of the stream had been opened and the bridges destroyed. "All that could be done was done." There was no personal attack against M. Reynaud, in spite of his speech of the 28th, or against General Weygand, in spite of the stinging message received the same day.

The impression, given by the King to the American Ambassador, concerning the differences which arose between him and the four members of his Government

who had remained in Belgium, reflects the same serenity: "They were all men of sincere motives. They did
what they did in the belief that they were acting in the
best interests of their nation. It was a sad thing that
when I left the country the Belgian people had passed
judgment on these patriotic statesmen without giving
their case a hearing." Compare these lines with those
which M. Cudahy wrote about the Sovereign himself:
"He suspected that his side of the case would never get
a hearing, that he would be in the position of a man
accused of felony who must listen to the accusing
testimony of the prosecution and be denied all defence." The conclusion seems obvious. If all the facts
were known, the accusations directed against the
Pierlot Government inside Belgium would appear as
unjust as the accusations directed against King
Leopold outside the country. Cardinal Van Roey
spoke of a "misunderstanding"; M. Cudahy, after
hearing the Sovereign, recorded a difference of opinion
between sincere men, anxious to serve the country and
to fulfil their responsibilities.

The date of the Cudahy interview is important. It
took place five days after the Ministers' visit to Wynendael, two days after the surrender, and three days before
the drafting of the memorandum which was later conveyed by the King's messenger to M. Pierlot *via*
Switzerland. It reduces still further the lapse of time during which the "misunderstanding" estranged the Sovereign from his Ministers. Everything seems to point to
the fact that, as soon as his mind was relieved of the
cruel anxieties caused by the military situation, the
King saw the tragedy he had experienced in its true

perspective. As Commander-in-Chief, he could not admit that his political responsibilities should interfere with his military duties. As prisoner of war, deprived of all power, he realized that his Ministers were entitled to fulfil their task. He also understood that the accusations levelled against him by M. Reynaud and Allied public opinion were the unavoidable consequence of his action, and he greeted them without any movement of revolt or righteous indignation. It was the price he had to pay for doing his duty. Calumnies followed him in his captivity as bombs had followed him in the field. The former attacked his reputation as the latter attacked his life. He might have avoided both by betraying his promise, he exposed himself to both by keeping it.

This immediate reaction was only to be expected from a man who had already given proof of a remarkable resilience of character. On the morrow of King Albert's death, he was found sitting at his father's desk. He resumed work at once after the funeral of Queen Astrid. He never relinquished his post for one moment during the '38 crisis, when war broke out, and during the series of alerts which kept Government circles in a state of tense anxiety before the invasion. In spite of his sensitiveness, King Leopold has inherited something of his father's stoicism. He knows how to take punishment, even if it is undeserved. If it had been more deserved, he might have been shaken by remorse; things being what they are, he is supported by the conviction of having done what he set out to do, to the best of his ability.

A few of his speeches have not been reported in the

Press. They were addressed to the clergy on the occasion of religious ceremonies and were only heard by a comparative few. They give us a glimpse in the King's outlook on life which may be valuable if we wish to understand his present state of mind.

On the anniversary of Belgian independence, six months after the death of his father, he said: "Happy are those who are able to turn towards our Lord, and find in their faith the courage to overcome the trials of life; and strong are those who can find in their faith sufficient energy to fulfil their duty." Two years later, on the same occasion, in Sainte Gudule, he recalled the words of Cardinal Mercier who exerted a considerable influence on his early training: "It is impossible to be a good Christian without being at the same time a good patriot." And he added: "The love of one's neighbours, the sense of duty, truth and justice, if applied to daily life, would spare mankind countless sufferings, troubles and anxieties. . . . The solution of the problems which oppress the world can only be found in the practice of Charity between individuals and between nations."

I still hear him when, at the close of the same year, he talked to me of his plans of economic reconstruction and of the urgent need for international co-operation. He alluded to the obstacles which hampered his efforts: procrastination, national selfishness, short-sightedness, and concluded: "Something should be done soon, for we are still at the mercy of an accident. We are living in very difficult times." I have given an account of this conversation elsewhere,[1] in which I

[1] *The Keystone of Europe*, pp. 351-356.

omitted one remark which I see no reason for omitting to-day: "And to think that we call ourselves Christians!"

I know that, in writing these lines, I am playing into the hands of those who scoff at any expression of religious faith. I do so deliberately, in the interest of truth, although this interest itself may be suspect to prejudiced minds. To associate religion with practical affairs, and Christianity with politics has become to some a proof of hypocrisy and to others a symptom of weakness. This "practical religion" must nevertheless be mentioned here, for it is the key to King Leopold's character and conduct as it was the key to his father's character and conduct.

The spiritual power which sustained the prisoner at Laeken during the years which preceded the invasion of his country will not fail him during his months of captivity. It will provide him with the inexhaustible energy enjoyed by those who, after making every sacrifice, are deeply convinced that, by persevering in the path they have chosen, they have everything to gain and nothing to lose.

5. *The King and his people*

When the Belgians heard M. Reynaud's speech, they were already plunged into a state of deep depression by the news of the military disasters experienced by the Allied armies. There had been no patriotic enthusiasm, as in August 1914, when Liège had inflicted a serious reverse upon the enemy. From the first, the vast majority of the people had been demoralized by the apparent invincibility of the invader, by the woeful tales of refugees, by the mass emigration of the bourgeoisie to France, and by the intermittent raids which held for them all the terror of novelty. The news of their King's treason announced from Paris with vociferous venom by the French Premier was the last blow. They were too stunned to think.

A few days later, Cardinal Van Roey's categorical vindication was read in every church. Those who did not hear it, heard the soldiers who had taken part in the last battle or read the accounts of the military operations. The reaction was instantaneous. Enthusiasm and loyalty surrounded the Sovereign, and M. Reynaud's bitterness was paid back tenfold. The hostility which his name provoked surpassed even that provoked by the Führer's.

King Leopold's popularity in Belgium during June and July '40, stands in violent contrast with his unpopularity in France, Britain and America. He was praised by the soldiers for having had the courage to fight to the last, and to take in the nick of time the decision which prevented a ruthless carnage. He was praised by the intelligentsia for having struggled so hard and so long to save the country from an unequal fight through which she could not be adequately supported, and for having gauged the situation prevailing in France, in spite of the illusions fostered by propaganda. He was praised by the women for saving the lives of their sons and husbands. He was praised by all for remaining with them and exposing himself to the same trials. Every reason given abroad for accusing the Sovereign of treason and cowardice was given in

Belgium for glorifying his loyalty and courage. Never did his reputation shine so bright among his subjects as when it was besmirched by strangers. Attacks from abroad only served to stimulate enthusiasm at home.

On the other hand, the members of the Belgian Government shared a great deal of the blame heaped upon M. Reynaud's head. It was enough to say that they disagreed with the Sovereign to condemn them outright. With complete lack of criticism, M. Pierlot's speech of May 28th was considered as a servile endorsement of the French Premier's utterance. His prolonged stay in France was more than suspicious. He had been "pro-Reynaud", he became "pro-Vichy". He was made responsible for the abuse launched against the Sovereign at the Limoges meeting. In short, M. Pierlot had his legend in Belgium as King Leopold had his legend in Britain, and these two legends were fostered by the same desire to find a scapegoat for the misfortune which both countries had suffered. The atmosphere was so tense that a certain number of Catholic and Socialist deputies, on their return from France, found it necessary to publish a letter to the King disassociating themselves from the attitude of their colleagues at Limoges and explaining that they had been "misled by the Government".

Needless to say, Nazi propaganda made the most of this situation. The King was eulogized by the German-controlled broadcast and by the Press, while every possible calumny was directed against M. Pierlot and his colleagues. Every attack made against the Sovereign, especially in London, was faithfully recorded in order to foster anti-British feeling. There was a deliberate attempt, not altogether unsuccessful, to enlist the Sovereign's popularity to the service of the "New Order".

The fact that the King did not accept any public responsibility and remained a prisoner of war and nothing else, checked this manœuvre and stiffened resistance.

This became apparent as early as July. The people had at first been impressed by the correct behaviour of the German troops. Somehow, the horrors of the *Blitz*, and the bombing of flying refugees had not provoked the same resentment as the deliberate arson and systematic massacres which had occurred during the first invasion at Louvain, Dinant, Andenne and many other places. The German soldiers' discipline was unimpeachable, and the authorities avoided the thousand vexations which had provoked such bitter opposition in 1914–1918. But it was soon made clear that if the appearances differed the intentions of the invaders remained the same. The forcible departure of the Ambassadors of neutral countries, the seizure of foreign and colonial stock, the war contributions and, still more, a succession of drastic requisitions of foodstuff and raw materials, showed plainly that Belgium was treated as an enemy country, and that her resources would be exploited to the sole benefit of the Reich. Further grievances were caused by the fact that the prisoners of war, instead of being at once released, were retained in German camps, week after week, and only liberated by small batches, in order to bolster up the blandishments of enemy propaganda. Distinctions made in this respect between Flemings and Walloons were resented by all. The encouragements given to the few disloyal Belgians who enlisted themselves in the service of the Nazis, and the repression of the first acts of sabotage added fuel to the fire.

The King's popularity remained the same, but Belgium and the preservation of Belgian independence once more dominated popular preoccupations. Tricolour ribbons were worn beside the badges with the crown and the letter L. Patriotic tracts and papers began to circulate secretly, as in the old days. In spite of Nazi regulations forbidding it, the anniversary of the Armistice was celebrated by crowds of people. In spite of Nazi regulations allowing it, the anniversary of the Sovereign was celebrated with the same fervour, on November 15th. An enormous number of bunches of flowers reached Laeken on this occasion. They came from all parts of the country and from all classes of the community. The figure of 250,000 has been quoted in this respect, but this must be a rough estimate, somewhat exaggerated either by the enthusiasm of the loyalist who spread the rumour, or by the exhaustion of the officials compelled to handle these floral tributes.

This change of mood had already begun to manifest itself before the mass aerial offensives directed against this country in August, but their failure, and the splendid resistance of the civil population to terrorism from the air, gave it a fresh impulse. British resistance revived hope in the future. It became once more possible to believe, not only in deliverance, but even in victory.

One of the arguments of German propaganda which did the greatest harm in France and Belgium was the well-known taunt that the "British were ready to fight to the last French and Belgian soldier." This argument had been strengthened by the reluctance shown in this country to make adequate military preparations in pre-war years, and by the fact that the uneducated classes were apt to estimate these preparations in actual troops, and to ignore the Fleet and Air Arms. It was now conclusively shown that the British were as good as their word, and ready to suffer for the cause they had chosen to defend. Pro-British sentiments revived rapidly and manifested themselves in many ways: the wearing of British colours, inscriptions chalked on the walls, or the laying of flowers on the British monuments. Such manifestations became so frequent in Brussels that the German authorities found it necessary to check them. Heaps of flowers laid in front of the Anglo-Belgian monument, Place Poelaert, were removed in November last. The authorities who had hitherto avoided such decisions made a first step in a direction which can only lead them to more unpopular repressions, and the Belgians to stronger resistance.

British successes justified the policy pursued by M. Pierlot. It was noticed that the King had never uttered a word against him and that, from the first, Cardinal Van Roey, who had been his interpreter, only mentioned a "misunderstanding" without questioning the Minister's good faith. Some of the refugees, after their return to the country, had been able to enlighten public opinion concerning the situation which prevailed in France at the time of the surrender, and the attitude observed by the Government in June and July. The breach between the partisans of the Sovereign and those of M. Pierlot was not yet mended but it was considerably narrowed and many began to see that there was no incompatibility between the attitude adopted by both sides. The debates of the Limoges meeting published by the *Nouveau Journal* in the hope of stirring indignation against the Government had the opposite effect, and M. Spaak's dignified speech, on that occasion, was compared favourably with those of the deputies who had blindly followed M. Reynaud's lead. The arrival of the Belgian Ministers in London, in October, further helped to clear the air. Opposition to the same enemy favoured the formation of a united front. Many of those who had regretted King Leopold's refusal to reign began to understand the reasons which prompted it, and were grateful for it.

By the end of December, the number of the Belgians who supported the Germans was reduced to a few agitators whose influence decreases in proportion to the support given them in the Press and on the wireless. While in 1916 and 1917, these agents were recruited mostly among the Flemings, they are now found in both parts of the country. It is comforting to notice that the Germans have not succeeded, this time, in exploiting language differences in the same way, partly owing to the fact that the reforms giving to both groups of the population equal standing had been applied for some years.

The great majority wish for a British victory, and

211

remain, at the same time, staunch supporters of the Dynasty. Some are prompted by a fervent loyalism to the Sovereign himself, others recognize that the preservation of the country's independence, after the war and in the event of an Allied victory, depends more than ever on the King's prestige and influence. Sentiment and wisdom point in the same direction.

6. *The King and Britain*

The feelings of Leopold III for this country are too well known to be emphasized. His school-days over here are not forgotten, nor the many friendships made in pre-war days. Although before and since 1936, the King deplored the slowness of British military preparations, he always realized that, in the future as in the past, this country would remain the main support of Belgian independence, and the strongest guarantee of its preservation. The King is well informed as regards Belgian history. Even if he were not, he could not forget the close connection existing between his own family and the British Royal Family, and the part played by England in 1831, 1870 and 1914. Without England, Belgian independence would never have been recognized or, if recognized, could not have been maintained for over a century in the most exposed corner of Europe. Without Belgium, Britain's security would have been threatened by the presence in Antwerp and on the Belgian coast of a great Power which, by seizing the keystone of Europe, would exert an unchallengeable hegemony on the Continent. Nothing which happened in the past or may happen in the future can alter this axiom of European history.

Judging from the serenity with which the Sovereign received the slanderous accusations launched against him all over the world, it seems scarcely likely that the campaign directed against him in England could have altered his opinion on this subject. He is not the kind of man to be swayed from a line of conduct by a personal grudge, or to sacrifice his country's interest to vindictiveness.

The future of Belgium is linked, on one side, with the future of the Dynasty, and, on the other, with the future of Britain. Without the King, there will be no internal cohesion, without a British victory, there will be no external independence.

It is most important, and even urgent, that this plain truth should be fully appreciated in British circles, and that those irresponsible speakers and writers who go on flogging the nightmare of the exploded Leopoldian legend should realize the harm they are doing, not only to the Belgian Sovereign and the Belgian people, but to the British cause. If they cannot be appealed to on the ground of truth and honesty, they should at least understand their own country's interests.

What are they hoping to obtain by pursuing their vendetta? It cannot possibly be the subjugation of Belgium, for in that case the hospitality given on these shores to the Belgian Government and the inclusion of Belgium among the "Allies", victims of Nazi aggression, becomes pointless. Besides, Lord Halifax, Mr. Chamberlain and Mr. Churchill have given all small countries of Europe, and particularly Belgium, the most definite and generous assurances of their restoration to a status of full independence. The independence of a people implies the choice of their Government. This choice, as far as the Belgians are concerned, was made in 1831 and has never been altered. The Belgians remain loyal to their Sovereign. Instead of shaking this loyalty, M. Reynaud has strengthened it to such a degree that the eventuality of the Sovereign's "deposition", suggested in France, in June '40, has become inconceivable to-day. It is difficult, in these circumstances, to understand why some people should persist in favouring Nazi tactics by vainly trying to estrange King Leopold from his subjects, and the Belgian people from the British Government. What purpose is there in aggravating a situation which is already sufficiently difficult, and in manufacturing unreal obstacles where serious obstacles already exist, and greater obstacles may arise in the near future?

I have spoken of the favourable reaction of Belgian public opinion towards Britain and I hope and pray that it will continue, but, as all occupied countries, and more than other occupied countries, owing to the density of her industrial population, Belgium is already exposed to severe hardships and may soon be threatened with famine. The Nazis, after requisitioning a large proportion of the country's foodstuffs, will put the blame on the British blockade and no doubt advertise, from time to time, the generous "gifts" they may be prompted to make in order to obtain the support of a starving population.

A great deal may depend on the manner in which this dangerous problem will be handled in Britain and America. Meanwhile, everything should be done to enlighten Belgian public opinion, and to counter by well-founded argument and, if possible, by some measure of practical help, the obvious manœuvre of the enemy. Nothing, on the other hand, should be done to confuse the issue and to weaken the country's resistance by manufacturing legitimate grievances.

The cause of King Leopold is inseparable from the cause of Belgium and the independence of a friendly Belgium remains in the future, as it has always been in the past, the bulwark of British security. It is in the vital interest of both countries that public statements made at a time when King Leopold's position could not be explained or defined, should be revised now that the facts are known, and that some public acknowledgment should be paid to the dignified and disinterested attitude which he has observed ever since the tragedy of May 28th, 1940.[1]

[1] Since these lines were written, at a meeting held at the Mansion House on May 29th, 1941, Mr. Eden, Secretary of State for Foreign Affairs, alluded to the "unbroken dignity" maintained by King Leopold. A month later, on June 24th, Mr. Oliver Lyttleton, then President of the Board of Trade, paid tribute to the King "for the example worthy of his father, which he had set to the Belgian people".

Chapter IX

A LAST TALK

MY FRIEND SAMSON had asked L. and me to dinner that night.

The sirens began to wail as we finished our frugal meal. We had been talking of the good news from Libya and Greece and, for the first time, the wary Samson had dared to prophesy: "If we can keep it up for another six months, the position will be completely altered. Hitler will have the war on two fronts which he has done his best to avoid."

At that moment, the *Blitz* began to roar overhead, a particularly heavy barrage with distant explosions which punctuated and sometimes interrupted our talk.

"What beats me," remarked L., "is the scorn poured on these Italian generals in Libya who are running away and leaving their troops behind. There is no logic in this world. Had King Leopold behaved in the same way, he would no doubt have been received here with open arms. They reviled him for refusing to do what these Italians are reviled for doing."

"Yes, it seems to have been a muddle," said Samson, "but we have some excuse for making it. The King's choice would never have let loose this storm if it had not been interpreted as a refusal to fight to the end."

"But there was no other end," exclaimed L., while something heavy dropped not very far away and the lights flickered ominously.

216

Samson was sipping his coffee in a meditative mood.

"Don't excite yourself," he replied. "It was excitement which did most of the mischief. And it is only calm and cool judgment which can undo it. I feel as you do that a grave injustice has been committed, that a brave and honest man had been wantonly dragged through the mud, and that those who accused him of treason, and I confess that I was one of them, have no leg to stand on now. *Now*, mind you. *Then* it was different. We had as much evidence to condemn him as any jury ever had to condemn a criminal, internal evidence, external evidence, circumstantial evidence."

"False evidence," added L., who could not restrain himself.

"Yes, false, but plausible, very plausible. It is all very well for you two who knew your King to blame me who was only vaguely acquainted with him through the gossip columns and the illustrated papers. Knowing him, when you heard Reynaud you did not believe your ears. Not knowing him, I did. That is the main difference between us. And, don't forget, you had nothing to say for months."

"One month, to be precise," I observed. "The memorandum of the three Belgian jurists reached London at the end of June. It clarified the legal situation—military surrender versus diplomatic negotiations—at the moment when the reports of the officers and men who came back from Dunkirk had already done a great deal to dispel false illusions about the state of affairs on the Belgian front at the end of May."

"Think also," added L., "of the effect of the French collapse in June and of the Armistice which followed.

217

Belgium could be excused for giving in after three weeks, when the best armies in France had not lasted a fortnight, and King Leopold's military surrender could scarcely be compared with an Armistice negotiated in spite of France's solemn pledge not to conclude a separate peace. Add to that the discussions provoked by Baudouin's attacks against the British in July, and the series of articles written in answer to these attacks by Senior officers of the B.E.F. These articles showed that the Belgians were entirely surrounded in Flanders, and that Weygand's plan came too late, at a moment when neither the British, nor the Belgians, still less the French, were in a position to put it into execution.

"Did you notice, by the way, how the comments made of the Belgian surrender improved as this fresh information came in. Lord Strabolgi's book appeared in July. He disproves the legend of treason, but his account of military events still bristles with inaccuracies picked up from hasty journalistic reports. Gordon Beckle's *Dunkirk and After*, issued a month later, shows already a considerable change for the better. The author had evidently been in contact with British soldiers who knew something of the situation of the Northern Armies after Sedan. But the first account of the Belgian Campaign which fits the facts was published by "Strategicus" in October[1] if I remember rightly. It deals adequately with the stories built on the banks of the Albert Canal with the supposed failure of the Belgians to "protect the left flank of the B.E.F.", and fully justifies the surrender from a military point of

[1] *War for World Power.*

218

view. Several well-known critics have followed the same line since. It needed four months to clear the air."

"You forget," objected Samson, "that these writers still dwelt, from time to time, on the burning question of no warning. That rankled in my mind long after I was persuaded that the Belgian Army had taken its full share of the fighting and had done its utmost to retrieve the situation, even after I realized that the King had no other alternative but to surrender."

"The Laeken memorandum which gives most of the facts," I explained, "could only be used in November 1940, five months after it had been prepared. My statement in the *Contemporary Review* appeared almost at the same time as Mr. Cudahy's articles."

"Why all this delay? Did you not realize that every week wasted could only be interpreted here as a confession of defeat, and strengthen public opinion in the belief that, if the Belgians did not speak up for their King, it was because they themselves had preserved some doubts? After all, if you did not show more zeal for such a good cause, how could you expect——"

Samson's voice was drowned by a tremendous crash. L. jumped from his chair.

"I am sorry," observed our host, "how inconsiderate of me! Would you prefer to go down? There's a shelter in the basement."

But L., shaking his head, went on pacing the room.

"My dear Samson," I said, "our friend is far less affected by that noise than by your quiet remark. You've touched a sore point. May I point out that the documents only reached London after a considerable delay. They were brought by people whose journey had not always been easy and who had to make considerable détours, experiencing a good many adventures on the way.

"There was another difficulty. Up to that time, the atmosphere had been anything but favourable. The legend had taken such enormous proportions in this country that any false move on our part—I mean on the Belgians' part—might have strengthened it instead of weakening it. When we had at last the facts, opinions differed on the use we should make of them. Some of us thought that we should wait for a change in public opinion . . ."

"A vicious circle," exclaimed L. "You wait for a change which can only take place if you do something . . ."

"Others," I went on, "as you may have noticed just now, wished to make a splash at once and give the documents the widest publicity at the risk of starting regrettable polemics. Others still, like myself, wished to act as promptly as possible, but to act discreetly in order to avoid rousing opposition, and to allow the truth to sink in gradually. I made some efforts, from time to time, in that direction . . ."

"Cudahy did more in a few days than you had done in a month," interrupted L.

"Quite so. But Mr. Cudahy was in a much stronger position. He was an American diplomat. He had seen the King since the surrender. He could give first-hand information. Besides, you will remember that his first attempt to right the ship was none too successful.

"He was accused of indiscretion and met with considerable criticism both here and in the States. It was only when he could publish all the evidence which he had gathered at Laeken that he spoke with authority and that his opinion carried weight. You cannot destroy a legend with mere assertions, you cannot oppose convictions based on truth to other convictions based on error. It is only in fighting false statements with reliable facts that you will clear the air."

"The same method should be applied against Nazi propaganda," suggested Samson. "The Leopoldian legend might have been invented by Goebbels. Nothing suited him better. His work is based on suspicion and doubt. After hearing him, if you don't know better, you feel inclined to doubt everything, even your mother's virtue, your King's patriotism. Goebbels revels in legends and it must have been delightful to him to see his worst enemies provide him with this one. On May 28th he must have thought that the Father of Lies had delivered his foes into his hands. He could assure the French that they had been let down by the British, the British that they had been left in the lurch by the French, and the Belgians that they had been slandered both by French and British. *Divide et impera.* What a beautiful piece of general disintegration! One thing was missing to complete the masterpiece, the figure of a loyal monarch, cornered into surrender, transformed into that of a low, lying traitor, selling the pass. Reynaud made him a present of it."

"And it has served him well," I added. "It has helped him to spread among the French, during the gravest crisis of their history, the feeling that they should trust no one, that the world was so permeated with evil that there was no loyalty left, that nothing mattered. It is still helping him to estrange some Belgians from the British by making them resent the attacks directed against their Sovereign in this country. Several of these attacks were carefully broadcast in Belgium by the Germans, and provoked an unavoidable reaction. A million refugees, soaked in the tense atmosphere of invaded France, may at first have been shaken in their loyalty, but the seven million Belgians who remained at home knew better. The tragedy is that, as long as the British legend against King Leopold is allowed to live, the German legend against the British cannot die.''

2. *Magna est veritas et prevalebit*

There was a lull in the *Blitz* during which L. resumed his armchair near the fire.

"What you said about facts and truth is not new," he remarked, "but it is very relevant in the present circumstances. I received the other day a postcard from a friend to whom I had sent some literature on this question. He is, by the way, one of the two or three finest historians in this country. It contained only five words: *Magna est veritas et prevalebit*.

"If I were in charge of propaganda, I should considerably reduce the time and space devoted to talks and articles exalting certain political ideals and systems, and reviling others. People have grown tired of listening to the personal views of the most eminent men. Ours is an iconoclastic age. You can defend systems or denounce them on various grounds, in various circumstances. Things change according to place and time. There is no universal panacea which can cure human evil and misery. But whatever you build must be built on a sound foundation. We are craving for reality. We want accurate facts put in their true proportion and perspective. We want sound principles founded on experience and a thorough knowledge of human nature. A statement is right or wrong, a thing exists or does not exist. That is the only sure ground on which we can fight with advantage the nightmare of fear, lies, doubts and suspicions with which our enemies try to surround us. In dispelling the Leopoldian legend, we help to dispel all legends. Truth is great and will prevail."

"All very fine, no doubt," objected Samson, "but must it prevail simply because it is true. Have not many false men succeeded and many righteous men failed?"

"I am dealing with societies not with individuals," retorted L., "and my standard is not merely the standard of worldly success. You may prevail in several ways. Since you are a Christian, I may remind you of the defeats which we suffer in this world and the triumphs which follow in another. This other world is with us all the time and it affects our social and political life. I take my last stand on the bedrock of spiritual and material reality. Truth is the holy ground where all those who have some decency left can still meet and join hands and fight together. I have renounced everything else whether you call it legend, dream or illusion."

"There are some beautiful legends," I mused.

"I was expecting that remark from you," answered L. with some acidity. "I know your fine distinction between good legends, based on truth, and bad legends

223

based on lies, but I do not believe in it. You are an artist and cannot give up worshipping your old idols. We have given up all that. This age is as hard in its virtues as in its vices. We have suffered too much from the consequences of your romantic dreams. The last century was full of them. See where they have landed us to-day."

"Art is not necessarily the result of wishful thinking," I objected.

"Nevertheless," broke in Samson, "I believe that our friend has hit the nail on the head. Truth must come first, the rest must follow. Man has been far too much inclined to twist the facts to suit his ideals instead of fitting his ideals to the facts."

3. *From prison to prison*

The bombardment faded in the distance, but an angry rumbling could still be heard from time to time. We settled in our chairs and lit our pipes.

"The more I think of it," I said, "the more the story of King Leopold appears to me as the story of a man, oppressed by his sense of responsibilities, who endeavoured to preserve his honour and reputation as every good monarch should do. In order to achieve this, as a boy, he submitted himself to a strict discipline, volunteering to serve in the trenches during the last war, pursuing his studies, travelling in distant lands, equipping himself physically and morally for the task he was called upon to fulfil. He had all the qualities required for the task. He was handsome, intelligent, a good speaker and, besides, endowed with a strong character. At one moment, it looked as if success

224

might crown his efforts. He married a Princess to whom he was devoted and who was devoted to him. As Heir to the Throne he was extremely popular. Belgium was proud of him. His star was rising. During this period, the influence exerted by King Albert cannot be overrated. He dominates the picture. The Prince's affection for his father was akin to hero-worship. His most ardent wish was to follow in the hero's footsteps. This attitude is maintained and strengthened after his accession. It shows itself in every word, in every action. It pervades everything.

"On the day of his accession the young Sovereign felt, no doubt, that the weight of responsibility had fallen too early on his shoulders, but he was comforted by the thought that his people readily extended to him and to the Queen the loyalty and devotion they had given to his father and mother. The tradition went on. He took his oath as the clouds were gathering over Europe. He swore to respect the Constitution and to safeguard the integrity and independence of the land. He "gave himself to his country", moved by an ardent and sincere desire to devote to his task the best of his energy, at whatever sacrifice.

"There is a strange mystery in a Prince's life which has often puzzled me. A statesman chooses his career. If, after his first success, he wishes to withdraw from the political field, nothing prevents him from doing so. If his public duties become too oppressive or intrude too much upon his personal interests, he is free to give up the struggle and hand over the keys of office to another. But a Prince does not choose. His family traditions, his training and education all urge him in the same direction. He is destined to reign from the cradle and when the call sounds he feels compelled to answer it. What is true of every Prince was particularly true of King Leopold, who had been brought up in the hard school of Duty.

"Under the Belgian Constitution, the Sovereign has a minimum of authority and a maximum of responsibility. No private misfortune can affect his work. Even the ghastly tragedy of Küssnacht is not allowed to interrupt the course of Belgian history. Eight million men, women and children are watching their King, praising him, blaming him, trusting him. And, on the horizon, the storm clouds are getting darker and darker and reach the Eastern frontier in March '36...

"He is in prison now at Laeken. He has been in prison for the last four years, always seeking a way out, and feeling the grip of iron tightening ever closer around this small, rich land which he loves, and these eight million people who, even if they criticize him, rely on him. A strong army and strong defences were the first safeguards required, and in order to obtain the means of building up this army and these fortifications he must alter his policy. "Prepare for war," says one voice. "Avoid war, at all cost," says another. He decides to do his utmost to prevent the conflict and, at the same time, to arm against it. Together with the best students of international affairs in this country, he has always believed that the greatest mistake made at Versailles, and more particularly in framing the Covenant, has been to neglect economics and to place the emphasis on politics. Economics should come first.

He develops this idea in letters and speeches. He knows that where there is no unemployment, where people are contented, the agitators and demagogues from the Right or from the Left cannot achieve power and threaten peace. He takes a keen interest in the van Zeeland report and gathers around him a number of experts. He dreams of founding an International Institute where the main economic problems which afflict the world might receive a temporary solution, apart from the turmoil of international politics. This came too late, of course, but whose fault was it? He did what he could, when he could, according to the modest means at his disposal.

"After Munich, there is a short respite. The King hopes against hope that something might emerge from 'appeasement.' He is not the leader of a great nation or in a position to create opportunities; he can only seize them as they present themselves to him in this relentless fight against the growing menace. He hastens preparations, relying on a defensive struggle. He asks for more guns, more planes. Where can they be bought? At what price? The blow falls before these questions are answered.

"See the prisoner, turning round and round in his cell, trying every lock, every bar in every window, while the walls seem slowly to close upon him. The small neutral States get together in August '39. He appeals to the Powers in their name. Then, with Queen Wilhelmina, he offers mediation, not once but twice. All in vain. He calls through the iron bars of his cell, but cannot make himself heard in the storm which is raging through Europe. The dogs of war are let slip, his voice is not strong enough to bring them back.

"Not strong enough? He has dared and dared. He has not shirked his responsibilities or taken refuge behind his Government. He is not weak of purpose, he has taken risks and exposed himself to fierce criticism at home and abroad. His weakness lies not in himself, but in the size of his country and in its position, on Germany's doorstep. His struggle is that of a resolute leader rendered powerless by circumstances over which he has no control. Belgium is now tossed about by the war like a small overcrowded boat in a storm. Still, he holds the tiller in a firm hand. There is nothing to do but to keep the boat afloat in the forlorn hope that the storm may follow another course.

"And, mind you, all the time, during these four years, during the Munich crisis, at the outbreak of war, during these scares which bring Belgium nearer and nearer to the catastrophe, he stands alone. Loneliness is the worst torture of prison life. His father has gone, Astrid has gone. He has only his children left and his widowed mother. There is no home life for him, no relaxation, nothing but the gnawing memory of a few happy years and the hopeless struggle round and round the silent and barren cell of his duty, of his honour, of his reputation.

"Mr. Cudahy saw him in January: 'His eyes were shadowed by the lack of sleep. Calm as he was, his hands betrayed the strain. . . . Strict neutrality had kept the war from the Belgian borders for four months, he reasoned, therefore it might keep Belgium from the conflict to the end. . . . Every day the

228

struggle was kept off Belgian soil was a day gained. . . .'

"The American Ambassador called on him again at
Laeken, in April, when the Dutch had had another
scare. The King told him that, from all the evidence
he possessed, he believed that this would prove another
false alarm. 'He hoped to make up for many hours
of lost sleep. He looked very tired, but more cheerful,
I thought, than at any former meeting.'

"On May 10th 1940, the final blow falls. It brings
with it a strange feeling of relief. At last, the King's
course is clear. He can step out of his prison and act.
After leaving no stone unturned to prevent the tremendous risks of this fight, he can wage it with a clear
conscience. The surprise attack on his first defence line
does not discourage him. His army is still intact behind
the 'iron wall' and the Allies are at his side. He takes
his orders from Gamelin. He is ready to play his part
at the side of Lord Gort.

"He plays it with skill and determination, and his
troops answer his call. They distinguish themselves in
an unequal struggle in spite of Germany's gliders and
tanks, and swarms of low-flying bombers. His lines do
not break, but France's do, owing to 'incredible mistakes'. They break right through from Sedan to the
Channel. He must obey orders, keep in touch with the
retreating B.E.F., and what is left of the French armies
in the North, abandon his 'iron wall', letting the
enemy enter Brussels and Antwerp, fall back first on
the Scheldt, later on the Lys. He is fighting now a
rearguard action in order to allow Weygand to launch
his counter-attack.

"Things are becoming desperate. His men are exhausted and their morale severely shaken. He has warned the Allies that he can hold on only for a few days. He holds on for a full week, knowing that all retreat is cut off. Every day, he expects better news from the South. Are the French coming? Will the R.A.F. bring at last to his men the feeling that they are not left at the mercy of the *Luftwaffe*, which goes on, by day and by night, dropping its bombs relentlessly, systematically over their lines? But the French do not appear. Weygand, instead of counter-attacking, is cutting his losses. The British are hastening their evacuation and the R.A.F. has too much to do elsewhere to be able to help the Belgians.

"Still, he has been told to hold on to the last and his duty comes first. In a final effort to keep things together, he promises his men that, whatever happens, he will stay with them. That Order of the Day stiffens their resolution, and gives the British and French a short respite. The circle of iron and fire narrows, the front is cracking in several places. The Belgians are now completely isolated and communication with British Headquarters has become impossible. After sending more warnings, seeing that a complete rout becomes unavoidable, if he attempts to pursue the fight, and that rout would involve a general massacre and throw the Allies themselves into confusion, the King at last lays down his arms. He might well have said, like Francis I: "*Tout est perdu, fors l'honneur.*"

"M. Reynaud will see to that," interrupted L.

"The story begins in a prison," I went on, "and it ends in a prison. It begins at Laeken, in March 1936, and it ends at Laeken, in June 1940. The first prison was the prison of adverse circumstances, the second prison is the prison guarded by German sentries. The King is as lonely and as powerless to-day as he was lonely and powerless four years ago, and he is as innocent of cowardice or treason to-day as he was four years ago."

"What a tragedy!" murmured L. "I wonder if it will ever be written."

"I hope it will," I replied. "I hope that, some time, at the end of this century, some poet will rediscover the story of King Leopold and transfer it on to the stage. It might be a solemn and soul searching lesson to the world. Oh! not on account of the legend and its false accusations. That will have been long forgotten. But on account of the contrast between the intentions of the man, his sincere and strenuous efforts, and the results achieved. The story makes hay of all the pious and sentimental twaddle which infects children's story-books and cheap novels, with their unavoidable happy endings. No, you can do your very best in this world, remain loyal to your friends, faithful to your undertakings; you can sacrifice your personal happiness and self interest on the altar of duty and honour— and you may fail utterly and completely.

"I am thankful that the King is a devout Christian. Christianity is the only thing which provides against such failures."

4. *Vindication and Panegyric*

"Since we are placing our problem in the pitiless light of Truth," said Samson, "I should like to ask you a question. Both of you have alluded again and again to King Albert and declared that he could not have acted differently if he had been placed in the same circumstances. Are you quite sure?"

"Yes," answered L., "he would have favoured the change in the country's foreign policy if he had been at the head of the State in '36. He would certainly have insisted on the necessity of strengthening our defences; he would have refused to enter into military conversations with any of the belligerents after neutrality had been declared; he would have done everything to prevent an attack against Belgium and to resist it once it had taken place. On May 10th, he would have placed himself at the head of the Army and endeavoured to defend national territory in close co-operation with the Allies. For all this, we have a series of precedents which are plain enough."

"I am more concerned with this meeting of May 25th with the members of the Government. I do not suspect the King's intentions but merely his wisdom. Had he not, at the moment, lost faith in any possible victory and was he not resigned to accept the consequences of defeat after having done his utmost to safeguard the interests of the Allies?"

"The position was not the same," replied L. with some heat, "and the comparison is not fair. King Leopold's decision to remain in Belgium was taken after the Allies had suffered a series of disastrous defeats. His retreat was cut off. The crisis in the 1914 campaign came after the victory of the Marne. The road to France was wide open and, although the fall of Antwerp was a catastrophe from the national point of view, it did not wreck all hope of pursuing the struggle on Belgian territory. Besides, the enemy's pursuit was delayed, partly owing to Allied intervention in Flanders. There was still time to reorganize the front for a last stand on the Yser. King Albert's situation was tragic enough, but cannot be compared with that in which his son was placed."

"My question," persisted Samson, "was not whether King Albert was placed in the same situation as King Leopold, but whether, knowing him as you did, you sincerely believe that he would have followed the same course if he had been at the head of the Army in May 1940."

"This question," I interrupted, "cannot possibly be answered, not only because we have nothing to guide us, but also because the strain which King Leopold had to endure was considerably more severe than the one his father had experienced twenty-six years before. The latter was never compelled to choose between his duty as Head of the Army and Head of the State. If you want my personal opinion, I believe that he would have sacrificed the second to the first, but that he would have prevented the misunderstandings which this sacrifice created in some Belgian circles.

"I do not wish to substitute one legend to another. It is one thing to declare that King Leopold has been the victim of the gravest injustice, that he remained loyal to his country and to the Allies to the extreme limit of human power, that he was neither a traitor, nor a coward, nor a defeatist, and showed himself an honest and brave man before and during the Belgian Campaign—and to say that he never committed any error, and that every word he uttered, particularly during the last crisis, was always inspired by a cool and perfectly balanced judgment. A vindication is not a panegyric.

"We know enough to say that the Reynaud speech was a political manœuvre and that the legend which grew out of it was merely the product of prejudice stimulated by nervous tension. We know enough to declare that King Leopold's intentions were as pure as the cause he defended, and that he defended it with devotion and energy. But we do not know enough to say that he always kept before him all the elements of the formidable problem with which he was faced and that he did not allow himself to be influenced by the cruel trials to which he was subjected. These problems and trials were such as to affect the strength of the staunchest fighter, not excluding King Albert.

"King Leopold, in his last decision, seems to have been guided by instinct more than by reason, an instinct which told him to place military honour above statesmanship, and to remain with those who were most exposed to suffering rather than to escape to a foreign land. He could not bear the idea of leaving his men and his people to the tender mercies of the enemy, and he brushed aside all other considerations."

"He chose the noblest course," interrupted L., "and made the greatest sacrifice."

"Patriotism is made of sacrifice," I went on, "but the highest sacrifice is not necessarily the highest form of patriotism. The future will show. You should place, on one side of the scales, the alleviation to the Belgians' privations and sufferings which the King may obtain by remaining in occupied territory and, on the other,

234

the alleviation to these privations and sufferings which
he might have obtained from Britain or America if he
had gone there. You should look, on the one side, at
the moral influence he may exert on his compatriots
by remaining with them and, on the other, at the
moral support he might have given to his Government
in pursuing the struggle. We are not yet and we may
never be in a position to appreciate the pros and cons
of this cruel problem, but they were worthy of serious
consideration and it appears, from our present information, that sufficient consideration was not given to
them. I am not prepared to go further than that."

"I am very glad that you go so far," answered
Samson, "and, to my mind, this strengthens your case
instead of weakening it. We are all human and as such
exposed to error, especially during a crisis. No one, in
this tragedy, seems to have been entirely above
reproach, and I cannot imagine that any one could be
among such catastrophic events. If you preserve this
attitude you will be in a far better position to dispel
the legend which, let me tell you, is still very much
alive.

"Only a few days ago, I saw your King's picture in a
popular paper, among those of the Sovereigns who had
'sold their crowns to Hitler'. I am afraid you do not
realize how strong are the prejudices which have been
aroused and how difficult it will be to remove them.
There is a natural tendency in man to believe in evil
more readily than in goodness. Once a reputation is lost,
it is not easy to recover. Once people have been led to
pronounce judgment, they are reluctant to recognize
their mistake. Besides, we are not living under normal

circumstances. Our thoughts are absorbed by new events and our fate depends upon them. Most of us have little time left to revise opinions which appeared self-evident at the time, and which still seem too plausible to be questioned. It needs a good deal of courage and humility to go back on certain pronouncements . . . "

"I thought," I interrupted, "that the English were less reluctant than others to acknowledge a mistake."

"I repeat, we are not living in normal circumstances. We are still waging a desperate war and our attention is centred in it. We have seen and we are still seeing so-called neutral countries giving way to threats and playing into the hands of the aggressor. We have seen and we are still seeing one monarch after another sacrificing the independence of his country in order to retain a shadow of power."

"But the surprise attack against Belgium and Holland," exclaimed L., "is the best proof that neither the one nor the other was ever likely to give way, and that Hitler had failed in all his attempts to lure them into his net . . ."

"I know, you have a strong case. I have heard it and I am more than satisfied. That is why I am urging you now to pursue your efforts, and not to blind yourself with the illusion that the battle is already won. Remember, you are rowing against the tide. I shall give you a few examples of what I mean. I have here Alexander Werth's book, *The Last Days of Paris*. Listen to this entry, dated May 28th 1940: 'God, I always thought Leopold a bad egg, pro-Nazi, pro-Degrelle, pro-Mussolini, and he did a lot of dirty work

236

during the Abyssinian business with his 'mystery visit' to London. The Hoare-Laval plan followed soon after. The B.E.F. people say he has a German mistress provided by the Gestapo—I heard them say so long ago.' . . . And further: . . . 'After all, Leopold mightn't have surrendered if Weygand wasn't staying behind the Somme; still it was a dirty trick to play on the French and British. Well, I suppose he'll be back in his royal palace complete with German girl-friend, etc. . . .'

"If these lines were written by an ordinary scandal-monger, they would only be the kind of stuff you might expect in the circumstances. But they were written by a competent journalist who enjoys among the members of his profession a well-deserved reputation of integrity. They reveal the intense prejudice existing in Paris at the time against King Leopold, especially in Left wing circles. They hated him as republicans, because he was a King, they hated him as Frenchmen because he had withdrawn his country from the ruins of Locarno, and they hated him as belligerents because he refused to alter his attitude before he was attacked. They hated him so much that they believed that he had come to London in 1935 to foster the Hoare-Laval plan[1] and that he had sold his country and the Allies for a mess of pottage, in the form of a German girl-friend 'provided by the Gestapo'. That, without this

[1] There is no foundation for this story. Even if there were, the worst that could be said against the King is that he shared the views expressed by Sir Samuel Hoare in his speech of December 18th. Belgium had agreed to apply economic sanctions, and her delegate had been one of the first to support the British Minister's strong attitude concerning collective security, at Geneva, on September 11th.

prejudice, Mr. Werth would not have lost his head is shown by the shrewd allusion to Weygand's failure to counter-attack. It was an obvious remark to make, but few made it at the time.

"Before I conclude, let me tell you a story. It will show you that I am taking my share of your labours.

"I went to a tea party last Wednesday. It was a rather smart affair and I did not see anyone I knew in the room, apart from the lady of the house. I was preparing to make my exit when I was stopped by a venerable dame in a green turban. 'I hear,' she said in a loud voice, 'that you take an interest in this awful man.' Her face was familiar to me, but I could not possibly put a name to it. I answered as quietly as I could, as I did not wish to attract attention, that I did not know whom she meant. 'Whom I mean?' she exclaimed in a louder tone. 'Leopold, of course. Tell me, how could he bring himself to do it? What's your explanation? I've an open mind, you know. Do you believe in this story of a Nazi mistress? Disgusting, I call it. Perfectly disgusting!' I whispered that I did not, and tried to worm my way towards the door. But she was too quick for me and intercepted me almost as I reached it. 'You don't? How interesting! Then, I suppose his Coburg blood did it.' I stopped at that and, placing one finger on my lips, I pointed out to her a member of the Royal household who was talking to our hostess only a few steps away. The lady turned pale. 'What is it?' she whispered. 'You should be more careful, my dear lady.' Suddenly the light of knowledge glared through her bulging eyes: 'Oh!' she said, 'I entirely forgot. Was that a *faux pas*?' 'After all,' I

answered, 'I seem to remember that the Prince
Consort . . .' 'This is terrible,' she exclaimed, 'do you
think she heard us?' 'She may have heard *you*.' 'Let
me remember,' she pondered, 'the great grandfather?' 'Exactly. And, in Belgium, Leopold I, the
great grandfather.' And, with this parting shot, I
made my escape.''

"You might have told her," laughed L., "that King
Leopold still wears the Garter.''

"I am glad you remind me of it," answered Samson.
"I feel sometimes that we are in danger of losing the
fine purpose for which we entered this struggle. This
lady with her green turban had accepted racialism as
a matter of course. Mr. Werth, on May 28th, was
carried away by political fanaticism. Others swallowed
blindly what they read in their paper months ago,
under sensational headlines, and cannot be bothered
to criticize these views in the light of present-day
information. Others still subject their moral standards
to the hard verdict of results. Success would have
justified everything. Failure condemns everything.
These are only slight and passing symptoms of the
grave disease which has spread over the Continent.
But, supposing we allowed them to develop, where
would they lead us?''

The "all clear" sounded at that moment, and the
clock struck twelve. We rose to go.

"There is a last question I wish to put to you," said
our genial host. "You spoke as if the story was ended.
But it is not ended. You say that, as long as King
Leopold maintains his present attitude, he will preserve the loyalty of his people. But will he maintain it?

He may be tempted to depart from it for many reasons, even for apparently good reasons. You have vouched for the past, can you also vouch for the future?"

"I stake my life on that," exclaimed L.

"And you, my friend?" asked Samson, turning to me.

"My confidence was not shaken when I received the news of the surrender at a time when I had absolutely no information. I fail to see how it could ever be shaken now."

"It is an act of faith?"

"If you wish to put it like that, it is. Doubts have done their evil work, it is high time that Faith should obtain a hearing. It is the only thing which can save Belgium."

"It is the only thing which can save the world," added Samson.

Outside, we strolled in the direction of L.'s flat, where it had been arranged that I should spend the night. A bright moon was shining and we decided to walk.

L. took me by the arm. "While we were talking," he said, "certain lines of Shakespeare came to my mind again and again. Let me think. . . . It begins: 'Who steales my purse, steales trash . . .'

"And it ends," I added:

'But he who filches from me my good name
Robs me of that which not enriches him
And makes me poor indeed.' "

"Thank you. Samson was right. What are we going to do about it? I don't like your idea of utter failure, without appeal, at least in this world. It is clear that the King sacrificed deliberately his reputation, his most cherished possession, on the altar of duty. But it is also clear that he did his best to vindicate it. Otherwise, why should he have written to the Pope and the President? Why should he have talked at such length with Cudahy? But what can he do? He is a prisoner."

"There was the prison of circumstances," I remarked, "and now there is the prison of misunderstanding. There are two prisons, one material, the other spiritual: Laeken and the legend. It will perhaps take as much time to deliver him from the first as from the second . . ."

"Because," urged L. impatiently, "you comfort yourself with the illusion that you have already done something."

"Perhaps," I replied, "or, with the illusion that, God helping, I might do something more."

And that is why this book was written.

I have done my best to state the facts of the case as fairly and dispassionately as possible. If I have not succeeded in showing that my King has been the innocent victim of a gross injustice, my efforts have been useless. If I have succeeded, I can only ask the reader not to play into the enemy's hands by blaming those who have, willingly or unwillingly, fostered the growth of the Leopoldian legend. I had no alternative but to expose these false accusations, but I am personally convinced that most of them were made in good faith, at a time when it was not yet possible to form an impartial opinion. I feel sure that the prisoner at

Laeken would be the first to blame me if I had only succeeded in vindicating him at the cost of more bitterness and recriminations.

It was in a spirit of charity that he sacrificed his freedom and reputation, and it is in the same spirit that he would wish public opinion to appreciate, not only his own words and actions, but also those of his worst enemies.

APPENDICES

I

King Leopold's Accession Speech, February 23rd 1934
(Extracts)

LADIES AND GENTLEMEN,

I do not underrate the scope and importance of the responsibilities I have assumed . . . in taking before you the solemn engagement which, according to the Constitution, seals a pact of mutual confidence between the Sovereign and the Nation . . .

Devotion to public duties has always been the character of the Belgian Monarchy. It was my Father's constant care. The fact that all Belgians understand the value of this close association between the Nation and its King explains the signs of affection which have been shown to us everywhere . . .

The wise institutions given us by the authors of the Constitution and which have been tested for over a century, are sufficiently broad and supple to adapt themselves . . . to the changing necessities of different times.

The King [King Albert] was deeply convinced of this, and . . . *I whole-heartedly share this conviction* . . .

The task of government is difficult during these times of crisis. Obstacles are accumulating on all trade routes. On several occasions, the deceased Sovereign emphasized this danger . . . I shall actively support all efforts aiming at developing agricultural resources . . . increasing employment, commerce and industry, and helping the middle-class and the workers to emerge from the painful situation in which they find themselves . . .

The country's independence and the integrity of her

244

territory are inseparable from her national unity. An indivisible and independent Belgium is an essential factor in the European balance of power . . .

Belgium will continue to associate herself with the organization of peace which she hopes will be maintained, according to the principles of honour and right, by closer co-operation between the peoples. She is resolved to make in the future, as she has done in the past, all the necessary sacrifices to safeguard her territory and her liberties . . .

LADIES AND GENTLEMEN,
I give myself body and soul to Belgium.
The Queen will help me, with all her heart, in the accomplishment of my duties. We will bring up our children in the love of the Motherland.

May Divine Providence assist us . . .

II

King Leopold's Speech to his Ministers, in Council, October 14th 1936.

SIRS,

When taking the Constitutional Oath, the Belgian Sovereigns swear to uphold the integrity and independence of the country.

Like my predecessors, I intend to fulfil this solemn promise. That is why I wish to preside at this Council which will take measures to be submitted to Parliament in order to give Belgium a military status adapted to the present circumstances . . .

It will, I think, be worth while reviewing the successive stages through which the military question has passed during these last months . . .

On February 7th 1936, the Cabinet agreed on the text of the Military Bill; *the latter did not receive sufficient support from the Committees of the House,* and the Government agreed to an amendment suggesting the immediate application of Article 53 of the Military Law.

The amended Bill was adopted by the House on April 6th.

Meanwhile, from January 10th, it had been decided that the problem should be discussed as a whole by a Mixed Commission. This idea was favourably received in all political and parliamentary circles.

The Mixed Commission which examined the problem in all its aspects, concluded its proceedings and issued a report of its findings.

These differ as to methods, but show a unanimity of opinion with regard to general principles. . . .

Confronted with the dangers of the international situation, the country would not understand if the Government were to delay in submitting to Parliament the most urgent measures proposed.

It is important that the problem should be carefully put before the public.

Our military policy, as our foreign policy, which of necessity determines the former, must be aimed, not at preparations for a problematic war, within a coalition, but at averting war from our territory.

The reoccupation of the Rhineland, in violation of the Locarno agreements *de facto* and *de jure*, almost brings us back to our pre-war international position.

Because of our geographical situation, we are forced to keep up such armaments as will discourage any of our neighbours from using our country to attack another State. In fulfilling this mission, Belgium contributes to a large extent to the peace of Western Europe; and, *ipso facto*, she earns the respect and eventually the support of all States interested in this peace.

I think that Belgian opinion is unanimous in this matter.

But our obligations should go no further. Any unilateral policy would weaken our position abroad, *and, rightly, or wrongly, stir up differences at home.* Even a purely defensive alliance would not achieve its purpose, for, however speedy would be the allied assistance, Belgium would immediately be invaded and ravaged. After this stage, friendly help might certainly ensure final victory, but in the fight the country would suffer such devastations as would make those of 1914–1918 pale into insignificance.

For this reason, as stated recently by the Minister of Foreign Affairs, we must pursue a policy "entirely and exclusively Belgian" . . .

Our military status, originating from the Military Law of 1929, excellent in many respects, no longer meets the new dangers of a lightning invasion. It neither insures the permanent defence of our frontiers, nor the safe mobilization and concentration of the Army. A more or less unexpected attack might, within a few hours, obtain invaluable advantages and irretrievably paralyze the bulk of our forces.

This deficient organization should immediately be corrected and it is in order to determine the means of correcting it that I have summoned you here . . .

III

Franco-British Declaration of April 24th 1937[1]

IN ACCORDANCE with instructions received from their respective Governments, His Majesty's Ambassador and the French Ambassador have the honour to make the following communication to the Belgian Government:

1. The Governments of the United Kingdom of Great Britain and Northern Ireland and of the French Republic have not failed during the last few months to give their full attention to the desire of the Belgian Government to have the international rights and obligations of Belgium clarified in certain respects where this is rendered necessary by her geographical position and by the delays which may still occur before the negotiation and conclusion of the general Act intended to replace the Treaty of Locarno.

2. The Government of the United Kingdom and the Government of the Republic, being anxious to give full expression to their sympathy with this desire of the Belgian Government, have agreed to make the following declaration:

3. The said Governments have taken note of the views which the Belgian Government has itself expressed concerning the interests of Belgium, and more particularly—

> (1) the determination expressed publicly and on more than one occasion by the Belgian Government: (*a*) to defend the frontiers of Belgium with all its forces against any aggression or

[1] British White Paper, cmd. 5437.

invasion, and to prevent Belgian territory from being used, for purposes of aggression against another State, as a passage or as a base of operations by land, by sea or in the air; (*b*) to organize the defence of Belgium in an efficient manner for this purpose;

(2) the renewed assurance of the fidelity of Belgium to the Covenant of the League of Nations and to the obligations which it involves for Members of the League.

4. In consequence, taking into account the determination and assurances mentioned above, the Government of the United Kingdom and the Government of the Republic declare that they consider Belgium to be now released from all obligations towards them resulting from either the Treaty of Locarno or the arrangements drawn up in London on March 19, 1936, and that they maintain in respect of Belgium the undertakings of assistance which they entered into towards her under the above-mentioned instruments.

5. The Government of the United Kingdom and the Government of the Republic agree that the release of Belgium from her obligations, as provided for in paragraph 4 above, in no way affects the existing undertakings between the United Kingdom and France.

Acknowledgment of receipt.

The Royal Government has taken note with great satisfaction of the declaration communicated to it this day by the Government of the United Kingdom of Great Britain and Northern Ireland. It thanks the Government of the United Kingdom warmly for this communication.

IV

Letter from King Leopold to M. van Zeeland,
July 21st 1937.

MY DEAR PRIME MINISTER,

When one considers the state of disorganization in which the world finds itself, one cannot but view the future with grave anxiety.

We should therefore strongly and earnestly encourage any attempt at organization which might further human solidarity.

Does not this thought emphasize the importance of the Mission which has been entrusted, through you, to Belgium, by Great Britain and France, and which goes far beyond the limits which are generally assigned to it, since it may lead to a search into the principles of a rational organization of world economics?

The welcome you have received beyond the Atlantic shows how well disposed are the United States towards the initiative taken by Great Britain and France. These three nations thus give us proof of their generous desire actively to help in the creation of a better order for which the whole world is crying out. The additional work which you have undertaken in accepting this great task will stir the gratitude of all those who understand its true aim and appreciate its vast possibilities.

As you are about to set out the preliminary results of your enquiry, may I make a suggestion? I think it would be essential to foster the creation of an institute of economic studies, the principal value of which would be its threefold character of universality, permanence and independence.

The object of its studies would be an enquiry into the elements of a universal economic organization and the adaptation of this organization to constantly changing economic factors.

Economic science is essentially living and subject to the rhythm of life. There can be no unalterable solution to its problems.

In order to fulfil its mission, the projected institute should be as independent as possible of national influences.

It is no doubt very difficult to separate economic from political questions, but it is precisely this difficulty which is the crux of the problem you are examining and on which we must concentrate all our efforts.

It is of the utmost importance that the institute should rely on the co-operation of those experts from all over the world, who possess the greatest knowledge of industry, commerce, agriculture, finance and labour. These experts should be chosen on their individual merit, and not as national delegates.

Neither the lowering of trade barriers, nor any half measure can alone put an end to the confusion which threatens peace. If we really wish to avert war and bring mankind to a more peaceful frame of mind, we must have the courage to face the economic problem as a whole, and to solve the major questions which threaten mankind: distribution of raw materials and means of exchange, international distribution of labour, relationship between agricultural and industrial countries, etc.

I am under no illusion as to the difficulties involved in realising this programme.

Nevertheless, I am convinced that this is a favourable moment to attempt it, and that we may hope, in furthering this effort, for the support, not only of all Governments, but also of the most important, social, religious and philanthropic bodies—in a word, of all men who desire and strive for understanding and solidarity. . . .

Believe me,

My dear Prime Minister,

Yours very sincerely,

LEOPOLD.

V

King Leopold's Hope

(The Times, November 18*th* 1937).

KING LEOPOLD has been welcomed in London with a
warmth which must have convinced him of the deep
sympathy felt in this country for him personally and
for his country. An exceptional cordiality has marked
the high traditional ceremonies of his reception—the
welcome on his arrival, the State banquet at Buckingham Palace, and the presentation of the address from
the City of London at Guildhall yesterday. . . . He is
accompanied by his Foreign Minister, M. Spaak, and
there has never been any doubt that they would avail
themselves of the opportunity to discuss the general
situation with British statesmen. In his reply to King
George's toast at the State banquet and again at
yesterday's luncheon, he showed that he hoped to see
Great Britain and the British Empire take the lead in
seeking for a solution of the economic difficulties
"which lie at the root of the international problems
which beset the world."

There was a frankness and directness in King
Leopold's references to this subject yesterday which
were peculiarly appropriate in a speech made in
Guildhall to his hosts, the City of London. We are
faced, he said, with a world problem which in its turn
is complicated by various national problems. Political
objectives are of concern only to certain sections, but
the better ordering of economic life is of interest to
mankind as a whole. The British Empire represents so
important a part of the human race that it cannot help

but realise more clearly than any other nation how closely the fate of mankind is bound up with its own. London is the financial, intellectual, political and economic centre of this Empire, sensitive to the anxieties to which the whole world is a prey. It follows that Great Britain has special responsibilities, and that the world is justified in looking to her to play a prominent part in finding a way out of the present difficulties. No one in this country will dispute King Leopold's diagnosis of the world's sickness. . . . His moving appeal will not fall upon deaf ears. An effective lead towards economic appeasement can only be given by Great Britain in co-operation with the United States. It is some encouragement to know that satisfactory progress is now being made towards the conclusion of an Anglo-American trade treaty, which is a necessary first step to co-operation over a wider field.

VI

Homage paid by M. Spaak to King Leopold in
Parliament (October 4th, 1938).

LADIES AND GENTLEMEN,

The other day, a Catholic journalist made an appeal for spiritual union. It has been achieved

Around the King, to whom—I shall not tire to say it —we owe a great deal, the King in whom all those who approached him, during these days of crisis, have found the same high virtues, the same calm courage, the same ardent patriotism and the same loyalty to the pledged word which made King Albert, in August 1914, the centre of our resistance,

Around Belgium, our Motherland, and all she represents through our institutions, our Christian and moral traditions, our sense of proportion, our love of liberty and peace.

Let this spiritual union be maintained.

VII

Extract from King Leopold's Speech, on October 12th, 1938, at the Unveiling of King Albert's Memorial Statue in Paris.

. . . .

Every man has his duties, every nation has its work. Belgium, situated at the cross-roads of Western Europe, has a mission of peace and mediation, a hard and heavy task, but how noble and worthy of un-ceasing efforts!

A cruel fate has, alas, turned her from her mission, and converted her too often into a vast battlefield instead of a friendly land, where nations could have met and peaceably solved their differences.

In order to accomplish their true mission . . . the Belgian people must assert and maintain a complete independence, as a symbol of their impartiality and the token of the confidence they wish to inspire. A policy of independence is not one of effacement and isolation. It does not disown the glorious memory of a recent past, nor the trials courageously borne with others. It implies . . . respect of the undertakings made by Belgium, within the limits of her power, faithfulness to the pledged word, loyalty and frankness to all, and it corresponds to her people's ideas of peace.

Quite apart from any threat of war, humanity is struggling in bitter strife in the midst of an un-precedented economic disorder which opposes and divides peoples, giving rein to egoism and hatred. Let us rise . . . above these jealousies and antagonisms, and resolve not to serve an abstract and sterile ideology, but to find a practical solution to these complex problems which impede the world's peaceful progress.

In order to win a fruitful peace, we must resolutely set ourselves to find the economic truth which can only be reached . . . by mutual confidence and active and patient co-operation.

The only way of establishing greater social justice, of apportioning to all the distribution of the world's goods, the just reward of their labours is to recognize this economic reality.

Reputation, whether derived from moral prestige or from material possessions, formerly the exclusive privilege of a few, becomes more and more the reward of those helpers of humanity who strive to create a spirit of brotherhood among nations which will exert its beneficent influence upon the economic life of the world . . .

VIII

King Leopold's Appeal for Peace in the name of the Oslo Powers, August 23rd, 1939.

(Extracts)

. . . . There is no country . . . who wishes to send her children to death, in order to take from other countries the same right of existence which she claims for herself.

Assuredly, the interests of States are not all the same. But are there any differences which cannot be better settled before than after a war?

Let the conscience of the world awake! The worst may still be averted. Time presses. The trend of events may soon make any direct contact still more difficult.

Let there be no mistake. We know that, in order to live, Right must rest on solid foundations, and the peace which we desire is a peace within the rights of all nations. A lasting peace can only be founded on a moral order.

Does not wisdom demand that we put an end to the war of words, incitements and threats, in order to discuss existing problems. We solemnly express the wish that those who direct the course of events should agree to settle their differences and their claims through open negotiations, in a spirit of brotherly co-operation.

That is why, in the name of H.M. the King of Denmark, the President of the Finnish Republic, H.R.H. the Grand Duchess of Luxemburg, H.M. the King of Norway, H.M. the Queen of the Netherlands,

H.M. the King of Sweden, and in my own name, each of us acting in agreement with his Government, I issue this appeal. We express the hope that other Heads of States will add their voices to ours, in the same concern for peace and for the security of their peoples.

IX

King Leopold's Broadcast Address to the U.S.A., October 27th, 1939.

(Extracts)

As I am convinced that my country is defending civilization by the attitude it has taken up towards the conflict that has broken out in Europe, I feel that I may limit myself to explaining the attitude which responds fully to the will, the courage and the honour of the Belgian people.

As Chief of the State, I am glad to have the opportunity of reviewing the following points:

In 1937, Belgium proclaimed her policy of independence and each of her three big neighbours acknowledged it. They went further, spontaneously gave us formal assurances that they would respect our frontiers and guarantee the independence of Belgium. The Belgian Government's declaration of neutrality, made at the beginning of the war, was the logical conclusion of our policy. . . .

We have no territorial ambitions. We are concerned neither directly, nor indirectly, with the origins of the conflict which divides Europe.

If Belgium became involved, her land would be turned into a battlefield; owing to her restricted area, her total destruction would follow whatever the result of the war.

Side by side with Holland, Belgium forms an islet of peace in the interest of all. Situated at the cross-roads of Western Europe, a neutral Belgium, loyal and strong as she is to-day, fulfils an essentially peaceful mission; she limits the extension of the battlefront and the distress of families. She constitutes . . . a citadel of peace and a means of conciliation which alone can save our civilization from the abyss towards which it would be precipitated by a general war.

We clearly see our duties and our rights; we await the future with a calm conscience; we are ready with all our strength to see that our independence is respected.

Exactly 25 years ago the Belgian Army, after a hard battle, checked, under the command of my father, King Albert, the progress of a cruel invasion.

If we were attacked—and I pray God this may not happen—in violation of the solemn and definite undertakings that were given us in 1937, and were renewed at the outset of the present war, *we would not hesitate to fight with the same conviction*, but with forces ten times stronger, and again, the whole country would be behind the Army. . . .

May I venture to hope that the American nation, to whom we are drawn by mutual aspirations and similar institutions, will help us and will support us in our attitude for the good of peace and the service of civilization.

APPENDICES

X

King Leopold's Proclamation to the Belgian People,
May 10th, 1940.

Belgians, for the second time in a quarter of a century, Belgium—a loyal and neutral country—has been attacked by the German Empire in spite of the most solemn undertakings contracted before the whole world. The Belgian people, who are fundamentally peaceful, have done everything in their power to prevent this, but *between sacrifice and dishonour the Belgium of 1940 will hesitate no more than did the Belgium of 1914.*

By awaiting the actual violation of our territory before appealing to our two guarantors, who have remained faithful to their promises, we have most loyally fulfilled to the last our duties of neutrality.

To our valiant Army, to our courageous soldiers, I address the greetings of the country. In them we place complete confidence. Worthy successors of the heroes of 1914, they will fight shoulder to shoulder to stop the onrush of the enemy through our provinces and to restrict the area of our national territory which is violated by the invader.

Thanks to the efforts which our country agreed to make, our fighting forces are infinitely more powerful than they were in 1914.

France and Great Britain have promised to help us. Their advance troops are already pushing forward to join up with ours. The fight will be hard. Great sacrifices and privation will be asked you. But there can be no doubt about the final victory.

I intend to remain faithful to my constitutional oath

to maintain the independence and integrity of the territory. *Like my father in* 1914, *I have placed myself at the head of the Army with the same faith, the same clear conscience.* The cause of Belgium is pure. With the help of God, it will triumph.

XI

King Leopold's Letter to H.H. Pope Pius XII, May 28th, 1940

Bruges, *May* 28, 1940

VERY HOLY FATHER,

In the midst of the general confusion occasioned by events through which we are living, moving with prodigious rapidity, and the import of which is incalculable, I desire to affirm that Belgium and her army have fulfilled their duty.

Belgium has upheld her international engagements, first in scrupulously maintaining her neutrality and then in defending, foot by foot, the entire extent of her territory.

Attacked by enormous forces, our army reached in perfect order a powerfully organized line of defence in liaison with the armies of the guarantors to whom we had appealed. But military events occurring outside our own territory forced us to evacuate this field of battle and necessitated a series of movements of withdrawal which pushed us back to the sea. There, our army spent itself, without counting the cost, in a four-day battle fought in complete agreement with the allied armies. We found ourselves finally encircled on an extremely restricted ground inhabited by a very dense population, already invaded by several hundreds of thousands of civilian refugees, who were without shelter, without food, without water and who were being driven about from one point to another by aerial bombardments.

Yesterday our last means of resistance was broken under the weight of a crushing superiority of troops and aviation. In these conditions, I sought to avoid a battle which to-day would have led to our annihilation without benefit to the Allies. No one has the right to sacrifice uselessly human lives. I intend to continue, whatever may come, to share the lot of my army and of my people. Requested for several days past to quit my soldiers, I refused this suggestion which would have been desertion on the part of the Chief of an Army. Further, by remaining on my native soil, I desire to stand by my people in the trial which they will have to go through.

The solicitude which Your Holiness has always evinced for Belgium makes it my duty to set forth to you without delay the reality of the facts.[1]

(s) LEOPOLD

[1] The above is the full text of the letter addressed to His Holiness the Pope. A similar letter was addressed by the King on the same date to the President of the United States. Both these letters were given wide circulation in Belgium.

XII

Pastoral Letter of H.E. Cardinal Van Roey,
Archbishop of Malines.
                    Read in all Belgian churches
                    on June 2nd, 1940.

OUR VERY DEAR BROTHERS,

The tragic trial through which we are going is being aggravated in the extreme by the very painful accusations formulated in Paris against His Majesty King Leopold III. These have painfully impressed the majority of the Belgian people.

In order to dissipate, if possible, the unfortunate misunderstanding, and to give, from a direct source, the clarification necessary, we deemed it our duty to call upon the Sovereign in person. The King was willing to receive us and has given us permission to make public the following statements:

1. The decision which he had to take, on the morning of May 28th, to lay down the arms of the Belgian Army was imposed upon him by a situation that had already become absolutely untenable. Irremediably surrounded, without hope of effective aid on the part of the Allies, our troops, if they had continued the fight, would have been handing themselves over to complete annihilation, without any military advantage, dragging to their fate hundreds of thousands of civilians crowded upon a tiny stretch of land.

2. This decision of an essential military order was taken by the King as Supreme Chief of the Army, in full accord with his Chief of Staff and following his advice. He has not performed any political act nor has

he concluded any treaty or pact—even of a military nature—with the enemy.

He acted because, corroborated by the unanimous judgment of three eminent Belgian jurists, he was convinced that he had the right to do so in virtue of the powers that the Constitution confers on the King in this matter.

3. It is contrary to truth to affirm that the Command of the Allied Forces had not been made aware of the necessity of ceasing hostilities. The odious accusation of felony is, therefore, false . . .

For our part, knowing that our sentiments are in accord with those of the almost unanimous mass of the Belgian people, we vouchsafe to our King our respect, our loyalty and our trust.

We ask our priests to continue reciting the liturgical prayers prescribed for the King . . .

We wish that all Belgians, aware of the gravity of the hour, remain united and firm behind the King, the supreme personification of our Motherland in danger. . . .

More than ever, let us confide ourselves to the infinite mercy of the Sacred Heart of Jesus, and let us say with the Psalmist: "For though I should walk in the midst of the shadow of death I will fear no evils, for Thou art with me." (Ps. xxiii, 4).

J. E. CARD. VAN ROEY,
Archbishop of Malines